CREATE

CREATE

A Simple Framework for Crafting Stories That Captivate, Persuade, and Inspire

ANNIKA UTGAARD

Booksmith Publishing

Copyright © 2018, 2020 by Annika Utgaard
All rights reserved.

Second Edition, Revised and Updated

No part of this book may be reproduced in any form or by any electronic or mechanical means, including information storage and retrieval systems, without written permission of the publisher, except for the use of brief quotations in critical articles and reviews.

Published by Booksmith Publishing | Seattle, Washington
www.booksmith.io

Trade Paperback ISBN: 978-1-7359725-2-7
eBook ISBN: 978-1-7359725-3-4

Library of Congress Control Number: 2020949494

Printed in the United States of America.

TO MY MOM,
for helping me reconnect with my inner child

I saw that my life was a vast glowing page, and I could do anything I wanted.

Jack Kerouac

Contents

Introduction	xi
1. Change Your Life…With a Book	1
2. Tell Your Story Effectively	16
3. Overcome the Desire to Procrastinate	29
4. Position Yourself for Success	40
5. Draft a Time-Saving Outline	52
6. Write the Damn Thing	72
7. Edit Like a Bestseller	82
8. Create Your Legacy	90
Conclusion	99
Resources	103
Leave a Review	111
About the Author	113

Introduction

> WHILE YOUR WORK IS GOOD, WE ONLY OFFER CONTRACTS TO AUTHORS WITH AN EXISTING FAN BASE. WITHOUT ONE, OUR COMPANY TAKES ON TOO MUCH RISK. FOR THIS REASON, WE ARE NOT INTERESTED IN PUBLISHING YOUR MANUSCRIPT AT THIS TIME.

READING THE WORDS of that letter, I felt my heart drop into my stomach. Frankly, I expected these rejections to become easier, considering how many I had received over the years. But they never did.

Each time I felt the sharp sting of shame and defeat, like a slap across the face. The suffocating fear of having failed as a writer swelled in my chest until I thought it was going to explode. Once again, I was struck by the all-too-familiar agony of getting close to the life I desperately wanted—foolishly believing that all I had to do was reach out and grab it—*only to find that it was still too far away.*

After the worst of the disappointment was over, I began the process of putting myself back together. I was quick to find some means of closure, as if a shattered dream could be pieced back together as neatly as the end of a novel. But real life is messy, and our dreams often end too soon, too late, or even in the middle of a sentence.

I had no idea what to do next or how to fix the situation. The only thing I knew for sure was that, despite what those letters said, this was still my BIG DREAM.

To become a published author...

To land a six-figure advance...

To see my books published alongside great writers like Paulo Coelho or Stephen King...

Not that I expected any of this to be easy; the road to authorship is long and full of dead ends. But after the latest rejection, I started to wonder whether the pursuit was still worth the heartache. How long would I have to endure the excruciating post-submission waits? Or wave after wave of rejection and disappointment? And what if no publisher ever gives me the chance to prove myself?

Well, to hell with that. I deserve better.

I deserved to have a publisher who would stand behind my work and help me connect with the right readers. And I knew that no traditional publisher could offer that, so I would have to do it on my own.

The old saying "There are plenty of fish in the sea" applies not only to the search for love, but also to the realization of our dreams. And in a world full of opportunities and different paths forward, I figured there had to be another way to become a published author. I just had to find it.

So, with my mind made up, I collected those rejection letters and used them to fuel the next chapter of my journey.

NOT SO LONG AGO, the biggest hurdle for any aspiring author was getting past the gatekeepers. This meant taking the time to put together a book proposal, along with a few sample chapters, before contacting dozens of literary agents. But instead of passing these proposals on to publishers, most agents would simply grumble that the submissions wouldn't make any money or be better off as articles in magazines.

For some writers, this was enough to abandon their dreams of authorship altogether. For others, who were more persistent, it was an invitation to send their proposals directly to the publishers themselves.

Writers can spend months, *even years*, waiting for a letter of rejection from a reputable agent or publisher. Most of the time, they don't even get a response. It sounds depressing, but for many it is the only known path to authorship.

The hard-to-swallow truth is that major publishers, including the Big Five, rarely pay attention to new writers. In fact, more than 99 percent of all submissions are rejected, largely because unknown authors lack an established fan base that can guarantee book sales. And, with the publishing landscape in a constant state of flux, book deals are becoming increasingly difficult to come by.

Before the internet, people went to bookstores to find what they wanted to read next, which is why having your book displayed on tables at BARNES & NOBLE was what sold the most copies. The idea was to maximize sales across physical retailers, and with the right distribution in place, traditional publishers thrived.

Then came the internet and, with it, the proliferation of social media. Suddenly, relationships between authors and readers were being built outside bookstores, leading more and more people to find their next book via online searches and recommendations from their social networks.

This shift posed a problem for publishers because they never had a relationship with the end customer (the reader.) Instead, they focused exclusively on expanding their network of brick-and-mortar locations. While the approach was not inherently wrong, their unwillingness to adapt to the changing landscape is ultimately what created a bad situation for business. As a result, the pressure to sell large volumes of books fell on the shoulders of authors. Thus, having a built-in audience or an existing fan base became the most important prerequisite for nabbing an advance and a publishing contract.

After learning this, I realized that there was no point in waiting years for someone to accept or reject my proposals and manuscripts. Considering that I would end up doing a good chunk of the work anyway, I figured, why not learn to navigate the industry on my own? Why not *liberate* myself from the gatekeepers of traditional publishing?

With this idea, I began to reach out to dozens of authors, especially those who had previously been published through traditional channels. I wanted to know what they thought about self-publishing. And you would not *believe* the exciting, even hopeful, conversations that the topic gave way to.

I discovered that the chance to publish what you want, when you want, in whatever way you choose, is the freedom that every author strives for. It returns both power and influence to the true creators of the content (not to mention 100 percent of the net royalties.)

What I also learned was that the stigma of self-publishing is quickly disappearing, even among the most established writers. The more I thought about it, the more it made sense. After all, there are many books that do not fit the traditional model, including those with:

- Niche topics that only appeal to certain groups of people
- Unusual formats or experimental writing for which an audience has to be created
- Authors without a "platform" or established fan base

And not only that: the business model and goals of an individual author are *completely different* from those of a large publishing house.

However, self-publishing is breaking down these barriers for writers. Add in the power and reach of social media, and it no longer seems far-fetched for aspiring writers to identify, locate, and connect with new readers en masse.

Whereas twenty years ago none of this would have been possible, today it is the new normal.

Between e-books, audiobooks, and print-on-demand technology, indie authors are quickly making traditional gatekeepers obsolete. Moreover, we now have multiple opportunities to build fan bases using online social platforms, which effectively levels the playing field. In other words, any indie author can develop her own publishing model, and the possibilities for doing so will continue to expand over time.

THERE ARE COUNTLESS dreamers and innovators out there who could do a lot of good if only they had the resources to make their ideas happen. That's why I firmly believe that books can act as catalysts to bring the right people and funding into one's life for that very purpose. All that's needed is a computer, somewhere to write, and an idea or two. Beyond that, it's a matter of taking the time to lay everything out in a way that others can follow and resonate with.

Every published book is an opportunity to increase the credibility and visibility of its creator, to establish more points of engagement for readers, and to open doors to real assets that can sustain the creator for years to come. The moment I understood *this*, I realized that the door to my dream of authorship would not be opened by traditional gatekeepers. Rather, I would have to create that door on my own.

And yet, I used to struggle with taking the ideas and stories in my head and writing them down in ways that made sense to others. In fact, when I first tried writing long-form content, I found myself trailing off into a bunch of unfocused nonsense.

It was only when I started experimenting with positioning and outlining that I realized how effective a structured writing system can be. Since then, I have developed an approach that has proven itself time and again, not only for me, but for many non-fiction authors. In a nutshell, the process looks like this:

Overcoming resistance. One of the biggest hurdles faced by most authors is when we sit down to write our books. Mental hang-ups and periods of self-doubt surround the creative endeavor and can quickly become a bottleneck in the process. To account for this, I discuss some tried-and-true strategies for overcoming various forms of procrastination and writer's block.

Positioning. In traditional publishing, positioning is intended to help authors figure out what results we want to achieve with our books, what specific audiences we should reach to get those results, and what value our books will deliver. I like to go a step further by helping authors identify what they want to do with their lives and how their book can steer them in the right direction.

Outlining. The outline lays the foundation on which authors build when we start writing our books. It organizes and structures ideas and stories in such a way that they make sense to the reader. It's crucial to take the time to get this step exactly right, which is why I break down the outline process to help budding authors advance the success of their narratives and drive results.

"Writing." Speaking, not writing, enables authors to extract the ideas that live in our minds and get them on the page with minimal effort. These voice dictations can then be transcribed and translated into the first draft of a book. Along the way, I share my secret for harnessing the power of story to open people's hearts and help authors stand out from a crowded and noisy world.

EDITING. To optimize the end result and communicate stories and ideas effectively, I apply a simple, two-step process used by all bestselling authors, enabling writers to minimize errors and nail exactly what we want to tell our readers.

By the time you reach the end of this book, you'll be ready to start the next steps in the publishing process. However, to avoid information overload, CREATE only focuses on the written aspect of book creation. If you would like a step-by-step plan for publishing and marketing your title, please read the next book in this series.

LOOKING BACK, I now recognize that those rejection letters never threatened my dream of becoming an author but encouraged me to create something even better. They inspired me to write this book and laid the foundation for my company, BOOKMITH.IO. So, in many ways, I should thank these publishers for inspiring my success. (Thanks guys!)

The point is this: *Just because the bar for publication is high does not mean that the path to getting there is singular.* In fact, the number of successes that any of us can experience over the course of our lives is as limited or unlimited as we make them.

At this very moment, dear reader, there is a whole world of possibilities on your doorstep, full of deeply passionate and powerful connections eagerly awaiting your arrival. But it is up to you, and only you, to write the book that bridges the gap between you and those possibilities. So, if you are ready to experience the life-changing power of transformative storytelling, then let's get started.

ONE

Change Your Life...With a Book

"A single dream is more powerful than a thousand realities." - J.R.R. Tolkien

MOST THOUGHT leaders have no idea how much becoming an author can change the course of their lives. From experiencing moments of catharsis to creating a legacy, turning your stories and ideas into a book is the perfect catalyst for launching the life you've always imagined for yourself.

Writing not only gives you the opportunity to share your vision for the future and your unique perspectives with others, it also attracts the right people to your mission because your story helps them understand what you do and why you do it.

After much trial-and-error in my own writing journey and after several conversations with other authors, here are a few key insights I've discovered when it comes to harnessing the power of storytelling:

JUST BECAUSE IT'S BEEN SAID BEFORE, DOESN'T MEAN IT'S BEEN SAID BY YOU.

The question comes up a lot for aspiring authors: *What do I do if someone has already written about my idea?*

Unfortunately, this mental hang-up appears all too often, and it causes us to stop pursuing something before we've even started. Why? Because we don't believe that we are qualified to teach someone else about it. This predicament can also occur when we feel that what we have to say is not entirely original.

To overcome this, ask yourself: *What perspective do you have that has been formed by your life experience?*

Being able to identify what's unique about what you've lived through is a good starting point because that perspective can be invaluable to others. Not to mention, no one else has been through the same set of circumstances that you have.

Each of us has been through hell at some point in our lives and lived to tell about it. But going through these painful moments is ultimately what expedites the learning curve, and the way we process the overall experience leads to the discovery of key insights that can then be shared with others.

In other words, two people can go through the exact same event, but interpret it in very different ways. So, if you are worried that someone else has already written what you want to write, please don't. Your perspective is unique to you, and you alone. As such, you should not hesitate to say what you need to.

Take Patrick, for example.

Patrick was a successful realtor, but he hired a coach because he wanted to switch careers and become a speaker. The problem was that he had no idea what he wanted to talk about on stage, and he was afraid of not being original.

During their first session, the coach said to him, "Look, as a speaker, the most valuable thing you have is content. But what makes your content priceless is when you turn it into intellectual property. The difference between intellectual property and the kind of content that everyone else has is your unique perspective, shaped by *your* heartache and *your* worldview."

The coach then asked Patrick to write down ten things that he thought, knew, or believed regarding a topic he was passionate about. Afterward, she asked him to read these ten things back to her. But something odd happened. As Patrick was reciting his list out loud, he began to yawn. That's when the coach stopped him and said, "If you're yawning, imagine how *I* feel. Why are you so bored?"

"Well, the first item came from Tony Robbins. The second one came from Oprah. And I think I took this third one from you."

The coach took the piece of paper from him and ripped it up. Then, she said, "Patrick tell me how you were wounded."

"Wounded? Like beat up on the playground?"

"Were you?"

"Yeah."

"Then let's start there."

That's when Patrick told the coach that, when he was growing up, kids had always thought he was crazy because he had a red wagon with an old copy machine. He would wheel the wagon around to local stores and merchants, and they would pay him a few pennies per page to make copies for them.

"That doesn't sound that crazy."

"Well, I got made fun of a lot."

"Who was it most painful to hear that ridicule from?"

Patrick took a deep breath and said, "My father."

"Okay, here you are. Present day. You're a wildly successful realtor. Tell me something crazy that you've done in the past year."

"Well, I bought a beer tap company that manufactures and sells kegs and taps."

"Okay, why?"

"I let my realtors give the kegs and taps out to their clients, and then they get invited to the parties. When people are tanked on beer, we get all the listings."

"How much did you make from doing that last year?"

"Over $1.5 million."

That's when the coach said, "I know what you should talk about."

Patrick gave her a funny look.

"Why not speak on innovation? You could completely blow up people's perspective. Be the guy that gives the crazy brilliant award to people like Tony Shay, who had the 'crazy' idea of selling shoes online. Redefine innovation and take a stand that being crazy is a brilliant thing."

Patrick's eyes filled up with tears. "I can't believe you took my greatest source of shame and not only gave me a path to healing it but showed me how I could use it to help other people."

Within one month of that conversation, Patrick was booked for a $25,000 talk. Instead of calling people up and saying, "Hi, I speak on innovation," he called them up and said, "I'm the crazy brilliant guy, and I'm going to show you how to *blow up* innovation."

The story that Patrick repeatedly told himself was, *I'm crazy, and I need to keep it a secret.* That's how he identified with it. Other people recognized that Patrick was a highly successful and credible businessman, but he had a slightly wacky side to his personality. And he only let that side out when it felt safe.

By revisiting this narrative—this piece of shame—from his childhood, Patrick was able to pick up the shadow of his former self, which was the part of him that was lost and buried deep underground. He had all kinds of resentment around being crazy, but when that worldview was tied back in with his brilliance, not only did Patrick feel validated, he also felt proud.

His big AHA! moment was, *This is who I am. I have a knack for this crazy brilliant way of thinking, and I finally found a way to use it to give back to the world.*

It's the classic hero's journey: One day, we wake up and begin to question our story and the trajectory of our lives. Maybe a significant life event occurs, or perhaps it's due to a prolonged feeling of monotony or restlessness. Regardless of the circumstances, when we question these narratives, we begin to integrate and learn from them.

The whole process can, of course, be a fine line to walk: being overly identified with your story means that you are a victim of that story. However, when you realize that your story is a core part of what has made you uniquely you, you can begin the journey of discovering the purpose behind it all.

The point here is that if you add your own twist to an existing concept or solution, no matter how great it already is, it becomes even better. By bringing your perspective and life experience to the subject matter, you allow others to directly benefit from your insights and apply these tidbits of wisdom to their own lives.

TAKEAWAY: Writing is about using your story to teach others something new. By weaving these two elements together, your readers get the information they were looking for and hear it rooted in human experience. This combination allows information to resonate with them in a way that it didn't before, and that is a very powerful thing. More importantly, your story builds a bridge between you and your readers. It's what makes people choose you over someone else, whether you want to provide a service or product, or even launch a new career.

THE PROCESS OF WRITING A BOOK HELPS YOU GET UNSTUCK.

We live in a society completely caught up in reality. We're so busy living off our clocks and calendars that many of us no longer remember what we grew up wanting to achieve. On the rare occasion that we *do* manage to come up with a creative idea or big career goal, the realist inside our heads pipes up with: *When are you going to find the time? Where are you going to get the money? What's the actual game plan here?*

Sure, reality plays a critical role in our future pursuits; however, being overly realistic tends to kill our passion and often leads us to believe that things need to progress linearly. We think that EVENT A needs to take place before EVENT B, which is not always the case.

Of course, there still needs to be a plan in place. Otherwise, the idea remains a fantasy, like winning the lottery. But if we jump to strategy too quickly, we often compromise our future ambitions down to what we believe is possible. For many of us, whether or not we take action is ultimately based on how much money we have in the bank.

I'm here to tell you that it is a myth to believe that things need to happen linearly. You can make significant progress on any dream in a short amount of time. The shortcut? Put your ideas into a book and share it with others.

Sharing your vision for the future creates momentum. The excitement builds and expands, as does your passion, when you spread the word to others. It also brings the right people to you instead of casting a wide net into the abyss and hoping for the best. These readers become your micro-tribe. Your cheerleaders.

Your ideas and insights are your magnets, and if you are effective in how you communicate them to others, you will be able to eradicate many of the obstacles related to money, or other resources, that currently stand in your way.

Now, to clarify, the best way to share your vision for the future (and get others onboard) is to write a book. Not just any book, but one that is carefully crafted to offer lots of value to its readers, creating maximum impact on both their lives and yours. We'll cover all of this in detail in the upcoming chapters. But for now, let me tell you another story:

Back in 2007, a football injury landed a 23-year-old guy on his sister's couch for a year and a half. He had no work experience, no college degree, and no money. Living off credit cards just to get by, the guy had no idea what he was going to do with the rest of his life.

Around Christmas time that same year, he read THE 4-HOUR

WORKWEEK by Tim Ferriss. As he finished the last page, he said to himself, *One day, I'm going to be friends with Tim Ferriss. I don't know how it's going to happen, but we're going to become great friends. I also need to figure out who his agent is because he needs to be my agent for when I write my book. It's going to be a bestseller and inspire millions of people around the world.*

At the time, this guy had no idea how any of this was going to pan out, and he has openly admitted since that writing has never been his strong suit. But he was willing to do what made him uncomfortable, every single day, to make all of this happen. And that was writing his book.

Fast forward eight years: He's good friends with Tim Ferriss, Tim's agent is his agent, and his book—SCHOOL OF GREATNESS—hit #2 on the *New York Times* bestseller list.

As you might have guessed, that guy was Lewis Howes, and he now runs *The School of Greatness* podcast, which shares inspiring stories from the likes of Danica Patrick, Gary Vaynerchuk, and Timothy Sykes.

Pretty cool, right?

When I first read about what he went through to get to where he is today, I wondered, *what makes Lewis Howes different from anyone else?* It took a while to answer, but here's what I came up with:

Lewis Howes chose to stop waiting for life to happen *to* him and started *creating* the life he wanted. He did this by sharing his vision with others. Many of us, on the other hand, tend to spend our whole lives waiting for our BIG MOMENT—the one that separates the life we are currently living from the one we wish to live. We wait around to become the person we always thought we were on the verge of becoming—holding out for the life we always thought we would have.

In our minds, we are always just one step away: In high school, we passed the time until we became the college version of ourselves. In college, we looked forward to the post-college adult that lay ahead: smarter, stronger, more organized. These days, we hope to be the winner of the next Powerball, or a bestselling author, or the founder of a major Silicon Valley startup. Why? Because *that* is when life will *really* begin. But days continue to pass us by, and we keep waiting for that time, that person, that event that will be our life's turning point.

Movies always portray this BIG MOMENT as the critical event that splits the timeline. It's the point where everything falls into one of two categories: life before the BIG MOMENT, and life after it.

That single moment changes everything. Sometimes, it's winning the jackpot or securing a seven-figure deal with Google. Other times, it's more personal, like meeting that special someone or losing 300 pounds. In any case, we all want this movie-worthy event to happen to us. Something that will change the course of our lives by pulling us out of the waiting game and into the adventurous life that we long for. But many of us go to work and come home and wonder why our lives don't look like the ones in our favorite movies.

> TAKEAWAY: Life is a collection of millions of little moments and choices. That BIG MOMENT that you keep anticipating takes a lot of time and effort and is often far less fabulous and dramatic than Hollywood leads you to believe. But that adventure, that movie-score-worthy experience is yours if you show up and do the work. Authoring your book is your BIG MOMENT—to impact lives, to be in the spotlight, to define who you are, and to declare yourself a leader. So, it's time to stop waiting and start working toward the life you truly desire.

BY SHARING YOUR IDEAS, YOU CREATE YOUR LEGACY.

I often meet brilliant people who are both knowledgeable and accomplished. They are full of innovative solutions and beautiful visions for the future. The problem is that their ideas are often reduced to casual conversations among friends and colleagues.

These individuals have undergone intense struggle and countless setbacks throughout their careers and private lives. And yet, they have emerged from all of this with a burning desire to use their stories to help others and positively influence the world around them. They only need a conduit for making that happen, which is why these thought leaders need to write a book. It's their opportunity to share their wisdom and perspectives in a way that adds value to the lives of others.

So, why don't they? Because, as human beings, we have a tendency to sabotage our dreams and do so in two major ways:

The first is by projecting our doubts and fears onto those dreams. All it takes is two quick words: *What if?*

What if I start a business, and it turns out to be a bad idea?

What if I move to a new country and end up all alone?

What if I go all in, write a book, and it ultimately tanks?

By front-loading our worst fears on to our future ambitions, we create a scenario in which moving toward these goals brings us closer to insecurity and self-doubt. To combat this tendency, we have to separate what we want out of life from everything else. This means that, instead of taking a reactive approach to our circumstances, we should consider a proactive approach. And, rather than just acting as problem solvers, we must become visionaries of what can be achieved by imagining the life we want and moving toward it.

As for all of those *what ifs* and *I can'ts*, remember that these thoughts are natural when you are pursuing something that lies beyond your comfort zone. The closer you get to your vision of the future, the closer you get to your worst fears in life, which is why it is important to distinguish between the two.

In other words, if you haven't dealt with your doubts and you meet a skeptic along the way, their doubt will only magnify yours.

But if you've dealt with those doubts, and you cross paths with that same skeptic later on, it becomes an opportunity to deepen your conviction and your commitment to the path you've laid out for yourself. And true visionaries stand up for what they believe in, even if they have to stand alone.

The second way we sabotage our dreams is by plopping them on our TO-DO lists. This is where long-term goals go to die.

Left in their raw state as simple inventories, TO-DO lists can quickly lead us astray. They inherently lack the intent of success. In fact, the only thing TO-DO lists are good for is getting you through your day-to-day life. What they aren't good for is making each day a stepping stone for the next so that you can progressively build a life of success.

For instance, you can't just plop the words WRITE A BOOK or START A BUSINESS on the same list that you're writing BUY GROCERIES or CLEAN THE APARTMENT. You need a separate list that is purposefully created to yield extraordinary results. This list should be reserved for taking you exactly where you want to go. It should be a place where you break down your big plans into smaller projects. Because nothing activates that inner voice of insecurity faster than saying you're going to do something and then not doing it.

To overcome this potential pitfall, break your goals down into projects that take one month or less. Because a month is short enough to stay focused and excited but long enough to where you'll see real results. And you need to see results in order to stay motivated.

I'll expand more on this point in CHAPTER THREE, but for now, know that the best way to reduce your risk of self-sabotage—and to lessen that dream's burden on your subconscious mind—is to share it with others. And do it with conviction because if you genuinely believe in the life-changing impact of what you want to achieve, others will too.

TAKEAWAY: If you want to create your legacy—something that is an extension of what drives you forward in life—you need a conduit for making that happen. Writing your book *is* that conduit. Becoming an author is a way to declare yourself a thought leader and add real value to other people's lives along the way.

YOUR BOOK IS THE CATALYST FOR LAUNCHING YOUR VISION FOR THE FUTURE.

You can make significant progress on any dream in a short period of time by authoring a book. Writing is just part of it though. To create the biggest possible impact, you need to have the courage to *publish* what you wrote.

Regardless of what you want to achieve, a book gives you the edge you need to grow and flourish as a thought leader and entrepreneur. In fact, here are some of the many ways this pursuit can act as your catalyst:

- **Be seen as the authority on your chosen topic.** From mountaineering to quantum physics, if you know something that is valuable, maybe even difficult to understand, then break it down and share it with the world. This, in turn, will significantly raise your visibility and enable people to recognize you for the thought leader that you are.
- **Launch a new career or advance an existing one.** By writing down your collection of relevant experiences and insights, you can expedite your climb up the professional ladder or switch careers entirely. In fact, if you don't love what you currently do, then you *should* author a book. Draw on your existing knowledge and write about a point of interest within your desired field.

- **Get paid to speak at events.** The moment you publish is the moment you are no longer part of the audience, but the person who is on the stage. Your book can be a very effective calling card in opening up all kinds of speaking opportunities. In fact, most organizations and conferences like to have external social proof that qualifies individuals for a specific topic before they invite them to speak. A book is a perfect proof that you know what you are talking about.
- **Generate inbound leads for your business.** A book is an excellent way to market your business, especially in smaller niches. Writing about what you do draws a ton of attention to your company from the very people you want to reach. Your book isn't just a fancy white paper; it's something that provides real value to your potential clients. This means giving away information and insights that you would typically charge for, to pull in high-quality leads who are right for you and for the services you provide.
- **Land big-ticket consulting clients.** When you tell people that you've written a book, there's a light bulb that goes off like, *Oh! Now I trust what you're saying a bit more*. It can be a very handy marketing tool and a perfect segue into landing you coaching clients and consulting jobs.

Now that you've seen some of the ways that a book can act as a catalyst for launching your vision for the future, let me tell you John Ruhlin's story, which demonstrates the impact of this process in action.

John is a born innovator. He started out as a knife salesman for a company called Cutco. But instead of taking the traditional door-to-door approach to selling knives, he met with CEOs and worked out a plan to send hundreds of custom knives to employees, vendors, and customers as a THANK YOU for their business. The strategy was a massive success, and John's career flourished.

Shortly after that, he developed a creative solution for corporate gift-giving that laid the foundation for his consulting firm. But while his clients thrived on his advice, John encountered a big problem: *Very few potential clients understood what he did or how he could help them.*

Many business owners understand the benefits of gift-giving, but no one could see why they needed to pay a consultant to assist them in the process. Furthermore, his existing clients had a difficult time explaining what he did and why it was so effective, so referrals were far and few between. John realized that if his clients couldn't explain what he did, then his agency had no chance of long-term scalability.

Instead of trying to change people's minds one-by-one, John decided to write a book so that he could spread his message on a larger scale. Additionally, John knew that sharing his ideas would allow those who couldn't afford his services to learn his methods directly and use them to make the world a kinder, more generous place.

Everything changed for John once his book, GIFTOLOGY, was published.

Before, his agency had received *some* media attention, but nothing substantial. Once he was published, however, John was able to land major media appearances in publications like *Forbes* and *Inc Magazine*, as well as podcast giants like *School of Greatness* and *James Altucher*.

The book also made John an in-demand speaker at several corporate events. He was able to nearly triple his speaking fees from $7,500 to $20,000 and ended up securing over fifteen paid appearances to discuss the ideas in his book—all within the first year of its release.

More importantly, the increased attention led to new clients for his consulting firm, Ruhlin Group. As a result, the agency prospered and grew rapidly. Prospects were able to find John and approach him for help with gifting. No intentional marketing efforts were necessary.

Giftology has become the ultimate tool for word-of-mouth marketing and an invaluable growth strategy for the Ruhlin Group. For John, publishing not only solved the major problem of scalability facing his consulting firm, but it also ended up being a success in several other ways as well. The icing on the cake, however, was that it represented a piece of him that had the potential to create significant impact for gift-giving in the corporate world.

Takeaway: Writing a book allows you to break down what you know, and what is relevant to your readers, so that you can provide both value and credibility to them. In return, this approach opens many doors for the future growth of your business or career.

As you can see, it's not a question of whether or not you have a great idea for a book, but rather, *are you ready to tell your story?*

If the answer is a resounding yes, then you are in the right place. The following chapters will dive into the art of storytelling, techniques for beating procrastination, the importance of laying a solid foundation, and how to write and edit your ideas into beautiful book prose.

If the answer is no, then this guide may not be right for you. And that's okay. Just put it down and walk away. No harm done.

If you aren't sure just yet, I encourage you to read on anyway. You might find that the process laid out here is applicable to other areas of your life or projects that you want to start in the near future.

In any case, I hope that the following pages will convince you that your ideas deserve to be heard and that the world is eager to hear them.

Now that you understand the massive impact that authoring a book can have on your life, follow me down the rabbit hole of storytelling and let's go lose ourselves in an adventure.

TWO

Tell Your Story Effectively

"We are, as human beings, addicted to story. Even when the body goes to sleep, the mind stays up all night telling itself stories." - Jonathan Gottschall

---

WHEN IT COMES to pursuing what we want to accomplish in life, it is essential to get other people on board. This is what makes the difference between our dreams taking off or disappearing into the sea of abandonment. This is also where learning how to communicate becomes so essential.

Storytelling is where history and human experience live. It's where tenacity, resiliency, and the human spirit are activated. The reason *why* you do what you do—that is your key to unlocking the door to your future.

What does this mean for you? Every single person in this world has a story that needs to be shared. It's not just about establishing an emotional connection with your reader; it's about helping people understand your *why*.

Why is this dream important to *you*?
Why should the reader choose *you*?

People choose people first, even before they decide to invest in their idea or business. If you want to invite someone to join you on whatever journey you are on, that person needs to know your underlying motivations—your *why* for embarking on that journey.

In a competitive and globalized world, your story is the one thing that sets you apart from everyone else, regardless of how qualified you are or how much experience you have. In fact, here is the kind of impact your storytelling abilities can have on your future:

Twenty years ago, Lisa Nichols had just $12 in her bank account. She was a struggling single mom, living on public assistance. Rock bottom had become her home, and she was doing her best to survive. Today, Lisa is a millionaire entrepreneur, a bestselling author, a humanitarian, and a motivational speaker.

How did she manage to turn her life around? *By sharing her story.*

In 2007, Lisa was on *Oprah*, alongside some of the most brilliant thought leaders on the planet. All of them had been co-authors of CHICKEN SOUP FOR THE SOUL. She was the youngest person on stage and had been in the industry the least amount of time. Lisa was the newbie, and she knew it. But she did one thing that no one else did during the show: *She gave people insight into what she had lived through.*

That was the pivot point for turning her life around. Lisa's story resonated with so many people that, within seventy-two hours, and without having any of her contact information on the show or up on the internet, she received 9,782 emails.

Before *Oprah*, Lisa was scraping by, unable to make ends meet. Three months later, those emails converted to just under $400,000 in income.

STORIES AREN'T JUST MEANT to be entertaining or to provide some form of catharsis. Those are only side-effects. What you have lived through is both relevant and necessary for making the world around you a better place. To use a metaphor: If the ideas and insights that you want to share are the bricks that help other people build the structures of their lives, then your story is the cement in-between that holds the whole thing together.

Even if money isn't your primary motivator in authoring a book, it's important to realize that when you serve more, share more, and deliver more, you earn more too. In fact, I can't think of a single business or personal vision where a great narrative won't elevate the outcome.

Keeping that in mind, let's talk about how you can use Lisa's method to create the most significant impact on your storytelling:

First, be willing to take a risk.

More often than not, we don't want to take risks and set limits on how deep a story will go. But by erring on the safe side, we end up omitting the part that will resonate the most with our readers—thus, missing the point of connection completely. To avoid this, we must be willing to take a risk by going deep into what happened while remaining clear and concise. How can you go deep?

By showing the reader, rather than telling them.

A great story shows, not tells what happened. This distinction is *the* game-changer for most people and businesses.

Many of us are willing to describe an experience objectively but may not be as open to revealing how vulnerable and human we felt as we were going through it. To give you an example:

> *There was a time in my life when things were challenging. I experienced a lot of rejection and there wasn't much hope that it would get better. Eventually, I had to find a new path for my career, so I decided to embark on a journey toward self-publishing.*

That was me *telling* you a snippet of my story. It's decent; you learn a bit about me. But it's also a bit vague. If I wanted to *show* you, it would go something like this:

> WHILE YOUR WORK IS GOOD, WE ONLY OFFER CONTRACTS TO AUTHORS WITH AN EXISTING FAN BASE. WITHOUT ONE, OUR COMPANY TAKES ON TOO MUCH RISK. FOR THIS REASON, WE ARE NOT INTERESTED IN PUBLISHING YOUR MANUSCRIPT AT THIS TIME.
>
> *Reading the words of that letter, I felt my heart drop into my stomach. Frankly, I expected these rejections to become easier, considering how many I had received over the years. But they never did.*
>
> *Each time, I felt the sharp sting of shame and defeat, like a slap across the face. The suffocating fear of having failed as a writer swelled in my chest until I thought it was going to explode. Once again, I was struck by the all-too-familiar agony of coming so close to the life that I desperately wanted—foolishly believing I just had to reach out and grab it—only to find that it was still too far away.*
>
> *[...]*
>
> *Not that I expected any of this to be easy; the road to authorship is often long and full of dead ends. But after the latest rejection, I began to wonder whether the pursuit was still worth the heartache. How long would I have to endure the excruciating post-submission waits? Or wave after wave of rejection and disappointment? And what if no publisher ever gives me the chance to prove myself?*
>
> *Well, to hell with that. I deserve better.*

Notice the difference in that second version. It's the same story, but it required me to paint a picture for you and bring you into that moment with me. That's because *showing* demands more. It requires us, as writers, to dig deep, be vulnerable, and take the reader into that moment with us.

So, show your readers what was going on your head, what you were feeling at that point in time. If you are willing to unpack the experience, you'll be able to captivate students, clients, investors, and anyone else you are trying to reach.

Think about what you want to share as a movie. When you watch a movie, the first thing you notice is that it sets the stage. You note whether the storyline takes place in the past, present, or future. And you figure it out by observing the details in the opening scene, such as what people are wearing or how they're talking.

Paint that same type of picture for your readers. Take them into that room—that environment—and set the backdrop. Show them what you were going through. Instead of saying you were *angry*, say something along the lines of:

The hair on the back of my neck stood up. I felt the fumes exiting my nose. I thought my chest was going to explode. I was about to say something that I would regret for the rest of my life.

That is how you show the reader that you were angry. Really take the extra time to go deep into those moments. Take a risk by bringing your storytelling to a level of true vulnerability. Because when you are willing to give more of yourself to your readers, they are willing to return the favor.

TO CREATE THE MOST IMPACT, USE DIP THEORY.

DIP THEORY is the technique that Lisa Nichols used on *Oprah* to get 9,782 emails from individuals who wanted her to coach them in their businesses. It's also what got the *Today Show* to call Lisa and ask if they could interview her. And here's how you can implement it in your writing:

Start by thinking of the letter V.

The top left corner of that V is your bio. Your bio is what you would say if someone asked you, *what are your qualifications? What makes you a credible source of information? What do you do?* Or, in some instances, *what is it that you **want** to do?*

Let's use Lisa's story as an example. For the top left corner of her V, she usually talks about writing seven bestselling books, being the CEO of a multimillion dollar company and having her brand known in 162 different languages. But don't worry if your bio isn't as glamorous. Just focus on the things, big or small, that show you know what you're talking about.

When Lisa was on *Oprah*, she didn't have a long list of qualifications. All she had really done at that point was contribute to the creation of CHICKEN SOUP FOR THE SOUL. So, what she did instead was use that contribution as her entry point—to leverage the credibility it gave her—before diving right into the bottom of her V.

The bottom of the V represents your all-time low. Your all-time low can be a challenging moment in your life or a difficult time that was significant for you. Take readers into that moment by showing them what it felt like to be there. This is where you allow others to see your humanity and to connect with you.

Just keep in mind that whatever moment you choose has to relate back to the subject matter of your book. So, if you are writing about financial freedom, talk about an all-time low that you went through financially. Don't talk about how your parents didn't love you enough.

Back to our Lisa example. This is how she approached her rock bottom:

> "There was a time when I was broke and broken. And being broke was easier than being broken. There was a time when I didn't have any money to put Pampers on my son. I had to sit and wrap him in a towel for two days. And I remember laying him on his back, putting my hand on his stomach, and promising him, 'Jelani, mommy will never be this broke again.'"

By describing that moment, Lisa made the audience feel like they were sitting on the couch next to her as she was trying to comfort both herself and her son. That was her all-time low, and it showed viewers that she was a real person, just like them. It tugged at heartstrings and established an emotional connection between Lisa and her audience.

The top right corner of the V is your WHY. Why do you do what you do? What is your inspiration? Why are you choosing to pursue this path? Why are you writing a book?

In Lisa's story, she talked about having no money, no Pampers for Jelani, and no food to feed him. That promise she made to her son demonstrated why she was committed to her work. But she also made a point to come out of the V—out of that low point—and leave her story on a positive note.

Lisa's goal in telling the audience about that moment with Jelani was to leave them feeling inspired. So, she followed it up by announcing her commitment, based on her journey through struggle:

> To touch as many lives as possible and to put the necessary tools in the hands of the audience so that they could create better futures for themselves.

People remember dips. That is how they connect with you and

your story. Dips are also how people remember the lessons that came out of those stories. They allow your readers to understand your *why* for doing what you do. If you just jump from who you are to your reasons for starting something, without providing any kind of dip, you will miss that point of connection with your reader entirely. If that happens, they will tune out whatever you say next as if it were background noise.

If you think about it, many successful people use dips to enroll others in their mission. (Think Elon Musk with SPACEX or Tony Robbins in his early twenties.) They don't just give us their bio and tell us why they want to teach us. They show us what they had to go through to get there. So, don't be afraid of your past struggles or wounds. Instead, use them as your fuel. Choose the moments you are ready to share and then use those to inspire others.

At the end of the day, your story never really belongs to you. It only belongs to you at the moment in which you are living through it. After that, it is up to you to craft it in a way that will serve others and help them get through their own plights in life.

ON THAT NOTE, IT'S ALSO IMPORTANT TO BE AUTHENTIC.

Never underestimate people's ability to tell whether or not you are making something up as a performance. In other words, your story has to be your own, not someone else's. It has to *cost* you something, meaning you have to be willing to say things that you may not be comfortable saying. Share the thoughts that you never thought you would share. Take readers to a place of vulnerability, discomfort, fear, shyness, even self-destruction. Walk them through those dark times with you.

Why is this an effective way of connecting with readers? Because you chose to open up and trust them with this part of your life. And in return, they will choose to trust you.

Think of it like this: your reader is a mirror. Whatever degree you are willing to put your heart out there is the exact degree to which your readers—who could be future clients, students, or investors—are willing to match you.

The great paradox of opening up with your story is that the more truth you share, the more likely people are to fall madly in love with you and become your biggest fans. You may think that it's not that simple or straightforward, but people place a lot of value on openness and transparency, especially in the world as it is at present. So, the more transparent you are, the more you will be able to use your truth as a catalyst for your vision, rather than treating it as a roadblock. And this will inevitably lead more people to say, *I choose you.*

Last but not least, use the three most effective words.

Readers come and go but what gets them to stick with you long-term is when they decide that you are part of their tribe. In other words, you understand them and what they're going through. This decision happens as a result of the parallels your story has to their own.

Going back to our V analogy, when you jump from the top left corner to the top right corner, you only get the people who are living up there. But the masses are in the middle. They aren't sitting at rock bottom; they are smack dab in the middle. So, you've got to go down and back again, picking them all up along the way.

The trick to doing this starts at the top left corner with your bio. Never start with *I graduated from...* or *I want to sit and talk with you, just give me five minutes to explain...* If you do that, you will lose your reader's attention almost immediately. And if you lose your reader, you lose the opportunity to help them. So, the three keywords to start with when talking about your bio are:

Even though I...

These three words tell the reader that something is coming after your bio, and they will be eager to hear whatever follows. Using this phrase is how you get your reader's permission to do the whole brag fest surrounding your bio because they want to know what comes after. Going back to Lisa's example:

"Even though I have six bestsellers, there was a time when I couldn't figure out what I was going to do tomorrow. Even though I'm a great CEO today, there was a time I was so broken that I would have been of no use to anyone."

See how that works? It doesn't change the story, but it does change how the reader listens to you.

A great thought leader, a great writer, not only controls the content of his book, he also controls how the reader listens to what he has to say. Therefore, it is your job to set your content up so that your readers have the right lenses needed to understand your story. That is your responsibility to them.

Now, in one of the emails that Lisa received, a woman wrote:

YOU REMIND ME OF OPRAH, AND BECAUSE OF THAT, I HAVE A HARD TIME BELIEVING THAT I CAN DO WHAT YOU'VE DONE.

Lisa's response? *Oh! Well, let me show you where I've been...* Then she wrote about her credit cards being declined, robbing Peter to pay Paul, her son's father going to prison, and how she was diagnosed as clinically depressed and prescribed Prozac.

The woman then emailed her back saying, *what do you recommend for me?*

She instantly became willing to be Lisa's student. But for a minute, Lisa's bio wasn't enough to qualify her to teach this woman, which is why she had to go to the place in the V where she could pick this woman up. And that place happened to be right in the middle.

Now, many of you might be asking, *how often should I use* DIP THEORY *when writing my book?*

While your story is compelling, it should only take up about five percent of your overall time with the reader. Otherwise, the conversation becomes too much about you.

Of course, it is entirely up to you *how* and *where* you decide to place it in the context of your book, but in my experience, the INTRODUCTION seems to be the best fit.

Your story is how you build that bridge between you and your readers. And once the bridge is established, you are in a prime position to teach whatever topic you had in mind. Furthermore, if you want readers to take a specific action after they finish your book, then create a dip. Show the part of your story that inspires action, then teach your audience what they need to know. From there, tie it all back together at the end, in your CONCLUSION, and call on the reader to take action.

Even though showing your story requires more words, the advantage is that you build a direct relationship with your target audience. And taking that extra step is what increases their willingness to stick with you and remain loyal fans long after they've put your book down. So, take a deep breath and pull back the black curtain for them: *What was going on at that moment? Where were you going? Where were your thoughts taking you?*

Yes, you will feel vulnerable. In fact, after you write it, you will wonder whether or not you should share it. If you feel afraid of people knowing this about you, publish it as fast as you can. Don't back away from it.

Bringing the application of these principles up one more level, let's talk about how your writing will bring your market to you, even if you and your reader are in two very different places.

Tell Your Story Effectively

In marketing, you have to know how to talk to people in such a way that they can find you and follow you. This is achieved within the commitment of purpose and the delivery of results, but your story also plays a vital role in this process.

People have choices. Your readers are looking for the results that you can give them more than they are looking for you. And there are plenty of other authors they can choose from. What would make them choose you over anyone else is that they feel connected to you and your brand, and that connection stems from your story and how relevant it is to your readers' lives. Once you've established that connection, it's time to deliver on your promise of valuable content and actionable results.

Remember, your story connects with your readers, but it also provides them with a lesson. It shows them how to get through their own hardships. Stories are critical to up-ing the necessity and urgency of the lessons derived from your personal experience. But it's important that you don't just end at any random place; you should always end every story you share in a crescendo. To do this, ask yourself, *what is the big takeaway here? How will this make the reader's life better?*

You have to take it back up to your readers because the story doesn't end with you, it ends with them. They need to be able to put what you shared in their arsenal and make it their own. So, use the takeaway to create a bridge from your life back to your content. It has to make sense and be relevant as to why it was placed in the book to begin with. Don't make readers search for the meaning behind the narrative; hand it to them.

KEY TAKEAWAYS:

- Your story is the glue that sticks all of your content together.

- Your dip is relevant because it picks up every prospective reader, client, and student you want to reach.

- What you have lived through is the very thing that sets you apart from everyone else. It defines your unique serving proposition.

- Weaving stories into your lessons and into your content will take your book to the next level.

Use this technique in your writing, in your book, in building your brand. Use it when you're talking to investors or enrolling others to work with you. Mastering the art of storytelling is all about being authentic, being vulnerable, showing that human side of you. And you can learn it by experimenting with different ways of weaving your personal experiences into your content.

Remember that mastery doesn't happen overnight. It demands hours of practice and many failed experiments. But, if you learn *how* to share difficult narratives with others, you will be able to realize your vision of the future and achieve your goals faster than you ever thought possible. In fact, sharing your story is one of the most effective ways to deal with any insecurities you may experience and help you work toward a life or career that exceeds your wildest expectations.

THREE

Overcome the Desire to Procrastinate

"Tell your heart that the fear of suffering is worse than the suffering itself. And that no heart has ever suffered when it went in search of its dreams." - Paulo Coelho

---

LIKE MOST PEOPLE, I enjoy reading about the various things I *could* do but have a hard time finding the motivation to *actually* do those things. Norwegians call this DØRSTOKK MILA, or "The Doorstop Mile." The phrase is used to describe the feeling of reluctance one experiences when first starting something.

Of course, we all love to set goals for our lives, our health, our careers. But it often feels like pulling proverbial teeth when it comes time to actually taking action. We'd rather do *anything* else, so long as it means we can delay things for one more day.

DØRSTOKK MILA can be applied to any area of life, whether it's switching careers, losing weight, even writing a book. The hardest part isn't doing the work. It's choosing to start and renewing that commitment to ourselves every single day without fail.

Since I didn't want DØRSTOKK MILA to prevent me from finishing my book, I decided to break the whole project down into a series of smaller, more manageable tasks. As Mark Twain once said:

> "The secret to getting ahead is getting started. The secret of getting started is breaking your complex, overwhelming tasks into small, manageable tasks and then starting on the first one."

Granted, there are no *specific* instructions on how to overcome DØRSTOKK MILA for writers, so I had to create my own unique set for this endeavor.

How did I decide which small project to tackle first? I asked myself, *what is the one thing I can do that will make everything else surrounding this book easier?* The answer: Gamify my writing and use those small wins to keep myself motivated.

A common assumption about writers is that they only work when inspiration strikes. But, in reality, all great writers follow a strict routine. So, I figured that if I turned my book writing endeavor into a game, I could establish a daily routine that would allow me to see the project through to the end. And, it proved to be a highly effective strategy—because routine leads to discipline, and discipline drives the success of our creative journeys.

Following this approach, I found a place to write and went there every day at the same time, even when I didn't feel motivated or productive. At first it felt a bit boring and I wasn't able to produce much of anything. But after a week, I noticed that this routine was having a positive effect on my ability to write *on demand*.

I discovered that writing at the same time every day prepares the mind for the kind of creative thinking necessary for great storytelling. In fact, the most successful (and disciplined) authors in the world are the ones who have trained themselves to make writing a daily habit.

Of course, there were still times when I found it difficult to write, but having a routine in place effectively trained my creative energies to kick in at the right time every day. It's a lot like meditation: You have to quiet your mind so that you can hear the inner voice of creativity.

Establishing a daily routine and following it religiously made it possible to listen to what my inner voice had to say and write accordingly. That's when I *really* started to make progress.

The next step was to exercise my creative muscle in an effort to become a stronger writer. To do this, I decided to pen a handful of fictional short stories. I told myself that if I could write fiction—which requires a high degree of imagination and creativity—then writing non-fiction would be a walk in the park. So I gave myself a month to churn out a new story every week.

The whole process was actually a lot of fun. In fact, I had such a good time writing fiction that I found it difficult to fall asleep at night. My thoughts would race with new plot twists and exciting ideas for character development. So much so that I would often say, *screw it*, and return to writing into the early hours of the morning.

After they were finished, I posted these stories online under a pseudonym. It was a small step, but it brought me closer to conquering that ever-present fear of sharing my work with others. It also made me more confident in my ability to write.

Although the stories themselves were only *moderately* successful, every download, purchase, and review gave me enough small wins to push forward. And before I knew it, the time had come to publish under my *real* name. So I turned to a social writing platform called MEDIUM.

For months, I had been lurking in the shadows of this online community, reading one inspiring article after another by my favorite MEDIUM writers. (People like Tom Kuegler and Nico Ryan.) Every time I read one of these articles, I felt an intense urge to write for the platform. But, up until this point, I had been hesitant to start.

Armed with my goals for this book, along with notebooks full of conversations that had transpired in previous months, I finally felt ready to go for it. Within a day, I had my first three articles written up and ready to go. I submitted them to the biggest publications I could find but heard nothing in response. So, I decided to try again. This time, I pitched smaller publications like *Post Grad Survival Guide* and *The Writing Cooperative*. To my surprise (and delight), my submissions were accepted and published shortly thereafter.

Some fun results followed: I gained 173 new followers in ten days and accumulated 5,978 views, 3,301 reads, 382 fans, and 2,183 claps. I also started getting mentions and feedback on my writing, which I took as a sign that I was on the right path.

While this might not seem like much in the grand scheme of things, these numbers are what enabled me to overcome that last bit of mental resistance. I also discovered that I could use MEDIUM to get feedback on sections and chapters that needed more work. Sticking with my goal of publishing one article a day, it didn't take long before the first draft of my manuscript was complete.

The point here is that, instead of seeing my book as a giant pain-in-the-ass and not wanting to deal with it, I chose to break it down into smaller tasks (e.g. daily MEDIUM articles.) Writing chapters in bite-sized sections like this made the whole endeavor unfold organically. It also helped me completely avoid any temptation to procrastinate.

For me, using a social writing platform like MEDIUM was the best approach to getting past the internal resistance that writers frequently encounter. It turned a serious and somewhat cumbersome project into a more playful pursuit. I highly recommend it to those of you reading this. And I hope that you will experience similar, if not better, results than I did.

Finally, to maintain my new daily writing routine, I made a promise. Using MEDIUM to hold myself accountable to my book worked beautifully...*most days*. But there were times where this approach simply wasn't enough. So whenever my progress began to stagnate, I would tell myself: *Despite not feeling inspired, I need to keep moving forward.*

Throughout my writing career, I've rarely encountered this problem in the beginning, or at the end, of working on a book. More often than not, I hit a wall somewhere in the middle, when I reach a crossroads that I can't find my way out of. In these instances, I force myself to remain at my desk and work my way through it, even if it takes the whole day. I do this because I know that if I give into the temptation to take a break or walk away—until the problem resolves itself—I won't return to finish the book for weeks or months, if ever.

Making this promise as my journey unfolded created discipline, and staying the course got me over any mental roadblocks that stood in my way. This, in turn, enabled me to see the creative endeavor through to the end.

The main takeaway here is that when you feel fear or procrastination get in the way of your writing, it helps to take a step back and identify exactly what it is that's scaring you the most. Then find a way to make that scary thing work *for* you rather than *against* you. Look at your fear from a different perspective, which is what I often tell my clients. In fact, these conversations tend to go something like this:

CLIENT: "I want to write a book, but I can't get myself to sit down and write it."
ME: "Why not?"
CLIENT: "I'm afraid that if I do, my book will end up being terrible."
ME: "What happens if it's terrible?"
CLIENT: "I'll end up looking stupid."
ME: "What will happen if you look stupid?"
CLIENT: "People will make fun of me, and then I'll feel ashamed."
ME: "Okay, let me ask you this: How stupid and ashamed will you feel if you *don't* write your book?"

CLIENT: "Probably more-so. I know it's a brilliant idea and writing a book has always been a big dream of mine."

ME: "Will your strategy of *not* writing your book, to protect yourself from feeling stupid and ashamed by others, protect you from feeling stupid and ashamed of yourself?"

CLIENT: "No..."

ME: "Since you're risking feeling stupid and ashamed either way, which version is worse? Trying to write your book, and it being terrible? Or never writing your book and having to live with the regret and shame of that decision?"

CLIENT: "Never writing my book and living to regret it."

FEAR IS all about how you choose to look at things. If you can view it through a different lens, you will allow the fear of *not* writing your book—the very thing that scares you—to fuel your pursuit of greatness.

Remember that as human beings, we have a tendency to freak ourselves out. Mention the words BIG and ACHIEVEMENT in the same sentence, and our first thoughts are things like *difficult to get there* and *complicated once you do*.

We immediately feel overwhelmed and intimidated by the very prospect of big success. We worry that success will bring with it all kinds of soul-crushing pressure and unprecedented amounts of stress. We worry that the pursuit will rob us of precious time with family and friends, and perhaps even compromise our health. We aren't even sure if we are *worthy* of success. Then, of course, there's the fear of what might happen if we make an attempt but fall short. All of this uncertainty causes our heads to spin and leaves us doubting our abilities and dreams.

By allowing ourselves to freak out before we even take the first step, we deplete a lot of the energy we need to write our book. This tends to be the case particularly when lying awake at 2 a.m. with nothing to distract ourselves. We wake up the next day, too exhausted to deal with the action required of the dream. So, unless you are going to get out of bed and do something about it in the middle of the night, do yourself a favor and don't fall prey to the fears living inside your head. Nine times out of ten, they are far more frightening in your mind than they are in reality.

When you decide to achieve your big goal in life, you do whatever it takes. Just like I did. Or, you could choose not to make a decision, roll over in your bed, and convince yourself that life is fine the way it is.

Sure, it's easier to lower our goals and trajectories because that's what feels safe. Staying where we are feels prudent. We tell ourselves, BIG is bad, and, *we should think smaller to protect ourselves from getting hurt*. But if we allow small thinking to take over, our biggest dreams and ideas will never see the light of day. And that is far more difficult to live with.

THE BOTTOM LINE: None of us knows our limits. Borders and boundaries may be clear on a map, but when we apply them to our messy human lives, the lines aren't so apparent. And, since no one knows the limits of his future achievements, worrying about them is a waste of time.

When you are able to accept that big thinking is about who you can become, you look at it differently. Bold ideas might threaten your comfort zone, but they also reflect the most meaningful opportunities in life. Believing in BIG ACHIEVEMENTS is what gives you the freedom to ask different questions, follow unconventional paths, and try new things. And that is what creates doors to possibilities that, until now, have only lived inside of your head and your heart.

Something incredible happens when you decide to say, *Screw it. I'm going for this.* Somewhere inside of you, a switch is flipped, and suddenly, the thrill of the pursuit overtakes the fear that's been holding you back all this time. When you realize that your freedom lies on the other side of your fear, you feel alive again. And I mean *truly* alive.

There are plenty of times when we get a brilliant idea and it pushes us into unfamiliar territory, which is why deciding to commit is so essential. If we don't commit, we end up falling prey to the fear that our dreams are impossible and that we should give up before we've even started. If we *do* commit, we make a major course correction to the trajectory of our lives and push to make things happen. In doing so, we bring those goals to life.

In other words, thinking big is what produces extraordinary results. So, don't fear BIG goals or BIG thinking.

Fear mediocrity.

Fear a wasted life.

Fear the lack of living to your fullest potential.

Because when we fear BIG, we end up working against it, whether we realize it or not. We either run toward smaller opportunities, or we run away from the big ones. And while we don't need to eliminate our fears completely, we do need to move past them. And to do that, we need to think BIG. Doing so allows us to experience a life in alignment with our vision for the future and, of course, see our books through to the end.

NOW, before we move on to the next chapter, I want to challenge you with an exercise known as the 100-DAY JOURNEY. This is something that I often use whenever I feel even slightly tempted to procrastinate, and it can be a great resource when it comes to dealing with your own DØRSTOKK MILA.

It all starts with a simple question: *What can you accomplish in 100 days?*

Could you make progress on some unrealized dream? Or launch a new business?

Could you learn a new language? Or finally write that damn book you're always talking about?

Who cares if it's any good? In the words of NIKE, *just do it*. Because 100 days of doing something that you've been thinking about, even if it sucks, beats the hell out of spending another 100 sitting around, thinking about it. It's also way better than feeling stuck, restless, and tired. And that alone makes it worth doing.

Now, back to the question at hand: *What could you do with 100 days?* More specifically, what needs to change in your life?

What are you putting off?

What can you chisel away at?

What might happen if you spend thirty minutes *every single day* in the pursuit of something new, different, challenging?

What if you took 100 of the tiniest steps in the direction of your dream?

But more importantly, what popped into your head or swelled in your heart as you read this?

There. That's what you should go after.

What is the point of this exercise? As human beings, we need meaningful pursuits. Without them, our lives feel empty and directionless. We need to go after the desires that live deep inside our souls in order to reach our fullest potential. The things that excite you are not random. They're connected to your purpose, and it's up to you to follow them. To quote Judith McNaught:

"There will be times in your life when all your instincts tell you to do something, something that defies logic, upsets your plans, and may seem crazy to others. When that happens, you do it. Listen to your instincts and ignore everything else. Ignore logic, ignore the odds, ignore the complications, and go for it."

Thus, the whole point of the 100-DAY JOURNEY is that it teaches us to push past our fears and tackle the urge to self-sabotage early on in the creation process. Perhaps those anxieties are related to writing or sharing our ideas with others or maybe they have something to do with the fear of big success (or failure.)

Whatever your unease surrounding the endeavor may be, by the end of this journey, you will find that it no longer holds the same power over you that it used to. And that will only deepen your conviction and commitment to your book going forward.

What are the guidelines of the 100-DAY JOURNEY?

Mission. You need a purpose, a vision for the future. So, pick the one thing that defines you and represents your ultimate goal in life. When you have an idea of what that might be, ask yourself, *what is my* WHY *for doing this?* Once you can answer that, write it down and revisit your WHY every single day.

Time. Whatever project you choose to tackle during this 100-DAY JOURNEY—whether it's outlining your book, authoring a few chapters of it, or taking on a different part of the creation process—keep in mind that it should only take thirty minutes or less. If you want to dedicate more time to these daily undertakings, feel free to do so. But you should aim for tasks that are tiny and achievable within a regular deadline. Completing smaller tasks and projects makes it easier to follow through and avoid burnout.

Stakes. You need accountability. Otherwise, it will be too easy to push the 100-DAY JOURNEY off to one side and forget about it altogether. The easiest way to establish accountability is to make a public announcement about your end goal, begin posting snippets of your book in an online community, or to work with someone like a coach. For example, you could write about *when* you plan to finish your book in your MEDIUM articles or on WATTPAD. Alternatively, you could pledge $100 to a charity if you don't complete your book within the 100 days.

Once you have your end goal for this journey in mind, it's time to figure out what your book should be about and how to use it to affect the most lives.

FOUR

Position Yourself for Success

"The role of a writer is not to say what we can all say, but what we are unable to say." - Anaïs Nin

---

AT THIS POINT, you probably have a somewhat loose idea of what you want to write about. However, if you still don't know or aren't sure, don't worry. In this chapter, I will walk you through how to settle on the subject matter for your book and how to position it in a way that will maximize your results and create the most impact.

BEFORE WE BEGIN: Many aspiring authors have more than one book in them. However, it's important that you don't try to cram everything you know into one book. It's far better to write several of them than to overwhelm your reader in one sitting.

With that said, this first method is a less formal approach, but it's one that I've seen work for a lot of authors. Here is how it breaks down:

First, identify a problem that has created a lot of pain for you.

Your pain is often what holds the key to your book idea. To demonstrate this, let's look at DRIVEN by Dr. Douglas Brackmann. DRIVEN teaches highly-motivated individuals to master their gifts in order to get what they want out of life. Dr. Brackmann originally wrote this book because he grew up with ADHD and was told that this would be a life-long disability. He refused to see it that way, however, and spent year after year seeking to understand his diagnosis and use it to his advantage.

After publishing his findings, Dr. Brackmann began training entrepreneurs, professional athletes, even Navy SEALs to perform at peak levels. To do this, he used the techniques that he had taught himself to compensate for his ADHD. Of course, this knowledge was initially meant to solve Dr. Brackmann's personal problem. But when he decided to share it with others, many people resonated with his story. As a result, he was able use it to build a successful business for himself.

Second, describe your approach to solving that problem.

In other words, how did you get through it? Exploring problems and painful experiences that you have personally lived through is how you find the exact book idea you need to write about.

For example, in HOW TO RUN AWAY FROM HOME AND BRING YOUR FAMILY WITH YOU, author Adam Dailey talks about how he sold his company to travel the world. The only problem with this dream was that he was married with four kids. Despite having a large family, Adam and his wife educated themselves and became experts on traveling with children. They then wrote a book detailing their experiences so that others, who found themselves in a similar situation, could do the same.

Third, ask the question: Does anyone else have this same problem?

If so, can your solution help them get through it? Share the tools and techniques that you have created for yourself with others.

In MEETINGS SUCK, Cameron Herold provides a detailed guide on how to run a business meeting. What prompted him to write a book like this? As Cameron was busy growing three multimillion-dollar companies, he found, over and over again, that vast amounts of time and money were being wasted. Why? Because no one knew how to run a productive meeting.

Since there were no good resources nor seasoned consultants to combat this kind of problem, Cameron set to work experimenting with optimization strategies on his own. Afterward, he began teaching them to his direct reports and saw the productivity of his companies increase ten-fold.

EACH OF THESE authors had a real problem facing him. And because there were no solutions available to them, they were forced to solve those problems themselves. Afterward, they chose to share their solutions, and their stories, with others by writing their books—and ended up creating their legacies in the process.

One reason these books were so successful is that their topics focused on something that the authors themselves had gone through. This ensured that they were offering real value to their readers *because* they had solutions to real-world problems, not theoretical ones.

The other reason these books did well is that they dealt with problems that others were facing. This meant that there was an audience ready to buy the books before the authors had started writing them. That being said, if you have first-hand experience with a problem that a lot of people share—and if you have a solution to that problem—then other people will most certainly want to know how you solved it. And that will ultimately lead them to buy your book.

Of course, solving problems is a tried-and-true method for finding your next (or first) book idea. But if you are looking for something a little more concrete and analytical—something that is directly tied to ROI—then this next method may be a better fit for you.

To determine what your book should be about, it's crucial that you answer the following questions:

1. Why are you writing a book?
2. Who will care about it?
3. Why will they care?

For a hundred years, in the world of traditional publishing, this process was called POSITIONING, and every agent had this discussion with publishers about a book before they sold it. The process has since been adapted so that positioning now serves the needs of the author rather than the needs of the publisher. I have also used this adaptation with my own clients time and again without fail. So, if you're ready to dive into the process of writing your book, then let's tackle these questions together, and you'll be well on your way to doing so.

FIRST QUESTION: WHY ARE YOU WRITING A BOOK?

In other words, what do you want to get out of writing this? What does your book have to get you to be considered a success? What end goal do you have in mind?

Ultimately, you want the book to be effective for you. By knowing precisely what you want to accomplish, you won't get bogged down by trying to be everything to everyone. Instead, you can focus on a specific plan of action that will get you exactly what you want.

If you have trouble coming up with a specific end goal, imagine the following scenario:

> *It has been one year since your book was published. What has happened over the last twelve months that made writing this book worth it to you?*

Did it help you establish yourself as the go-to authority in your field?

Did it allow potential clients to find you and ask to work with you directly?

Did it land you one or two $25,000 speaking gigs?

Did it get your brand massive media attention from magazines like *Forbes* and *Entrepreneur*?

Did it take your company from struggling-to-make-ends-meet to generating an annual six- or seven-figure revenue?

Did it give you the opportunity to share your ideas and insights with people who used them to turn their lives around?

There are many, many things a book can get you. And no rule says you can't go after multiple results at one time. There can be overlap, so don't limit yourself to a prescribed number as you begin to evaluate your options. But *do* decide on at least one or two end goals before you move on to the second positioning question.

SECOND QUESTION: WHO WILL CARE ABOUT THIS BOOK?

Another way of putting this is, what group of people do you have to reach for these end goals to materialize? Whose support do you need to turn your pipe dream into a reality?

Remember that the audience you need to reach is directly tied to the results you just chose, and you can reverse engineer those results to determine exactly who your audience is. The key is figuring out who needs to know about your book to make it a success. This process is as simple as asking, *who has to know about my book for it to get the results I want?*

Be specific here. Saying that *everyone* is your audience is never an answer to this question. *No book idea appeals to everyone.* In fact, casting a wide net by writing on a broad subject is only marginally appealing. This is because broad topics, like general life advice, tend to not only be well-covered already but are also not very actionable for people. A focused book, on the other hand, holds far more appeal because it creates a lot of value for a smaller audience.

For example, it's easy to determine the ideal reader for a book that lays out how non-profit organizations can set up successful fundraising campaigns. Even though it's a very niche topic, the people who pick up that book are going to be very interested in benefitting from the author's experience and expertise. Compare this to a book about a broad, general topic, like how to be happy. You might *think* everyone cares about being happy, and that is true to some extent. But unless you are already an expert on this subject and have an angle that has never been explored before, it will be tough to convince people that *your* book about happiness—as opposed to the seventy books already out there by other experts—is the one they should read.

As you consider who will care about your book, also take some time to get clear on your secondary audience. In other words, who knows someone who could benefit from your insights or become an avid supporter of your mission, vision, or ideas and share them with others?

Think of it this way: The subject matter directly affects your primary audience, whereas the secondary is indirectly affected by it. While the secondary audience is interested in the topic itself, it likely affects them to a lesser degree.

THIRD QUESTION: WHY WILL YOUR READERS CARE?

What problem have you faced and found a solution to that your audience will care about? What do you have to say that could help someone else get through something similar?

This final piece of the positioning puzzle can be tricky and often overwhelming for most authors. You know what you want to get out of writing your book—and you have a pretty good idea of who you need to reach with it—but the last question is what determines whether or not you have something worth saying. And it isn't always easy to answer.

By pulling your ideas out of your head and getting them onto paper, you are defining everything that you are about—who you are, what you've been through—as well as your unique beliefs and life perspectives. Because of this, the whole process can leave you feeling vulnerable, especially knowing that, in the end, you'll be sending this personal creation out into the world and exposing it to the judgment of your peers.

That said, writing can also be a very cathartic process. Creating, in general, is cathartic, but putting your ideas into a book is how you connect all the dots in your life and establish your legacy, which is why this last question is so important. So, let's take some time to break it down further:

Start by describing the avatar of your primary audience. Think of someone specific. Who is this person?

It's useful to define an avatar because it helps to imagine your ideal reader. For many authors, this is the first time they've considered the perspective of their audience. They've only imagined the reaction someone might have to their book and haven't spent any time thinking about *why* they might react that way.

Think about what it's like to decide on the next book you want to read. Do you ever think about the author or their problems? Of course not. You think about why buying that book might help *you*. So, pick a specific person. It can be someone you know personally or some fictitious character that accurately represents the person you want reading your book. Create a vivid picture of this individual in your mind. Who is she? What does she look like? What are her interests? What happens in her day-to-day life?

What headache or heartache is this person experiencing because he or she hasn't read your book?

People pay attention to stories, especially stories that resonate with their problems, pain, and internal conflicts. Once they are in touch with those pain points, then they want to hear about solutions that provide relief and pleasure, and maybe even take them somewhere new in their lives.

You are writing a book because you understand what this person is going through. You've been where she is now—to hell and back—and lived to tell about it. Do you recall what it was like? What about this particular headache or heartache gives you something in common with this person? Bring yourself back to that low point in your life and reconnect with the thoughts and feelings that you experienced during that time. This is how you establish an emotional connection with your reader.

What benefit will this person get from reading your book?

Now that you've pinpointed your reader's headache or heartache, think about what you know now and how that knowledge can guide this person through their ordeal. How will reading your book help this individual move past her problem? How did *you* get through it? What do you know now that you wish you had known back then?

Remember that no one else has the same set of life experiences and perspectives that you have, so the way you solved this particular pain point is probably something that no one else has thought of before. Identifying what your approach was and the mindset that carried you through it is exactly what your reader needs to hear. That is the benefit, *the hope*, that your book has to offer. It's what creates value for your readers and sets you apart from everyone else. Establishing that connection is how they relate to you and is ultimately why they choose to engage with you later on.

ONCE YOU HAVE ANSWERED these questions, the key is to check all of them against each other. If you don't have anything relevant to say to the audience that you need to reach, then you need to re-examine your book's objectives in order to reach the readers that you can help. Alternatively, you may need to narrow your goals even further so that you can find an audience that is easier to reach.

> HOW IT ALL TIES TOGETHER: Your end goals create your reader. The reader has her needs. Your book provides a solution that meets that reader's needs, creating huge value. This allows you to achieve your own goals as a byproduct.

To demonstrate this process in action, let me show you how I positioned CREATE:

FIRST QUESTION: WHY AM I WRITING A BOOK?

1. To inspire thought leaders and aspiring writers to harness the power of storytelling, while giving them the right tools and techniques for success

2. To launch a publishing services platform that helps indie authors navigate the confusing landscape of publishing and marketing.

SECOND QUESTION: WHO WILL CARE ABOUT THIS BOOK?

My ideal readers will resonate with the book because they:

- Feel overwhelmed and frustrated by the book writing process
- Want to harness the power of storytelling and experience life-changing results
- Have no idea how to structure ideas and narratives in a way that makes sense to readers
- Want a system that makes it easy to write a book as efficiently and painlessly as possible
- Need help expressing thoughts and ideas in a clear and effective way

WHO IS MY SECONDARY AUDIENCE? *Who knows someone who could benefit from this book or become an avid supporter of my mission, vision, or ideas?*

People who know someone who should write a book but keeps putting it off. They are interested in helping this individual share their ideas with a core group of readers and experience life-changing impact as a result.

THIRD QUESTION: WHY WILL MY READERS CARE?

There are many dreamers, innovators, and aspiring writers who want to create their legacy—something that is an extension of the dreams that drive them forward in life. This book will help these individuals communicate their ideas and stories so that they can achieve that goal.

By following a simple process for positioning, outlining, writing, and editing a book, readers can avoid the major pitfalls that surround the creative endeavor. More importantly, they can focus on expanding their ideas in a beautiful, meaningful way that resonates with others.

Describe the avatar of the primary audience. Think of someone specific. Who is this person?

Elizabeth is a 45-year-old who recently decided to switch careers. After a disappointing experience with a professional fundraising firm, Elizabeth feels that her organization was taken advantage of. After doing some research, she is frustrated that there are no better alternatives in the local area.

Lately, she's been taking online courses that focus on fundraising for nonprofits and decided to start her own consulting business. However, since her background is mainly in marketing, Elizabeth needs a way for organizations to find her and view her as a fundraising expert. She has heard that writing a book can help her overcome these hurdles, but isn't sure how to go about it.

What headache or heartache is this person experiencing because she hasn't read my book?

Elizabeth doesn't believe she has the time, discipline or motivation to sit down and write. Moreover, she feels overwhelmed and frustrated by the process. She has no idea what to say or how to connect with her readers.

Elizabeth is also wondering, *what if my ideas aren't original? What if someone else has already written about this before?* These thoughts make her feel stuck and ready to give up before she has even started. Worse, she doesn't know that there are resources available to help her navigate this process.

What benefit will this person get from reading my book?

Reading this book removes Elizabeth's pre-existing paradigms surrounding the traditional approach to non-fiction writing. She now has a guide for authoring a book on her own; a step-by-step infrastructure that she can work with right away. She also knows that there are people out there who can help her through the post-writing process if she doesn't want to deal with the publishing and marketing side of things. More importantly, Elizabeth understands that her book can act as the catalyst for launching her new consulting business.

In becoming an author, Elizabeth experiences a moment of pride and excitement when the first copy of her book arrives. Holding it in her hands, she realizes that this book defines a pivotal moment in her career and in her life. It is her way of declaring to the world that she is a credible thought leader.

BY ANSWERING these questions before you start writing, you are setting yourself up for success and will find the rest of the process much easier to work through. So take some time with your positioning, as this is the foundation on which you will build.

Once you are confident in your answers, it's time to move on to laying the groundwork for your book.

FIVE

Draft a Time-Saving Outline

"I had nothing but an old typewriter and a big idea. And so rock bottom became a solid foundation on which I rebuilt my life." - J.K. Rowling

AT THIS POINT, you should have a good idea of what results you expect from your book, what audience you need to reach to achieve those results, and what your book should focus on to reach that audience.

The next step is to organize your ideas into a structured outline. This is where all the heavy lifting happens so that you are well-prepared to start writing in the next chapter. It's crucial to get your outline just right, as it allows you to understand the logical flow of your ideas. That being said, it's best to do this in steps, starting with the bones of your book and building that skeleton out into a full outline. Don't worry though. We'll go over all of these steps, in detail, before I cut you loose.

WHY BOTHER CREATING AN OUTLINE?

Yes, it sounds tedious and probably isn't how you want to spend your Saturday afternoon. But, even though outlines take some effort to build out, there are numerous benefits to taking the time to create them. One of those benefits is that it allows your writing to stay focused and enables you to dive deep into your subject matter. It also makes the writing process much less frustrating, as it saves a lot of time later on. Ironically, the more effort you put into the outline, the less the reader will notice or become aware of the organization, which is exactly what you want.

Imagine you are building a house. If you want to start from scratch, you will probably work with an architect. And when you talk to the architect, you begin to brainstorm ideas. The architect's job is to take your ideas and desires and structure them into blueprints. He then draws up these plans so that the general contractor can follow them when building your house.

If you apply the same concept to your outline, the structure that you create now lays the foundation on which you will build when you write your book. That said, it's important that you understand the structure of your house, like what size it should be, how many bedrooms you want it to have, where the kitchen is—things of that nature. This will give you the big picture of how your book should progress.

What you do not need to specify at this point is what color you want to paint your house or what kind of countertops it will have, which is the level of detail you get into later in your writing.

The goal here is to create order out of your ideas in a way that makes sense to the reader. Your job is to be both an advocate for your audience as well as the author of the story you're telling. As such, think about what you would want to know, clarify, and understand if you were a reader. But be careful not to exhaust yourself at this stage of the process. Don't write down everything you know in your outline because you will end up having to do it over again when you begin to write. Just put down enough details to jog your memory.

BEFORE WE BEGIN: It's important to do this right. Don't rush anything because, again, sticking with the house metaphor: *If you pour a bad foundation, you are going to have a bad house.* Spending time now to make sure you solidify all your ideas—and that your subject matter is exactly what you want to publish—is super important. It's easy to make changes at this point but, later on, it will be more difficult.

Now, let's go over how to build out your outline in detail. First, we'll get into some of the high-level content, which should give you the information you need to construct a SKELETON OUTLINE. A skeleton outline is just what it sounds like: the very roughest bones of your manuscript. After that, we'll dig into the details and start to flesh out what will go in each chapter. This will be the INTERMEDIATE OUTLINE. Once that's finished, all you have to do is fill in any remaining gaps in content.

If everything is done right, you should be able to move on to the writing phase. However, if you experience any hesitation along the way—about whether you're going in the right direction—then stop and take the time to make the necessary adjustments before moving on.

THE SKELETON OUTLINE

WHEN CREATING THE SKELETON OUTLINE, your primary objective is to be naïve and approach the subject with a beginner's mind. In fact, you should be thinking on the same level as an eight-year-old here, by asking a lot of questions, like, *why is that?* This approach allows you to fully develop your thinking in a way that makes sense to, and resonates with, your reader.

During this stage of the process, you want to focus on two key areas: 1. *Explain the problem you are solving* and 2. *Explain the solution you are offering*. Understanding these two elements is what gives you the bones of your book. Now, you can choose any structure that feels right for you, but the most basic arc for non-fiction books is:

Problem Statement → Explanation → Solution

A more fleshed-out version might look like this:

- Compelling opening to grab attention
- Pull the focus back to a more general problem statement
- Introduction of solution
- Development and explanation of solution
- Circle back to connect solution to problem statement
- Call to action

In general, a skeleton outline should contain enough information to understand the narrative arc and logical flow of your book, while also making it easy to identify problems, if there are any. With that in mind, here is a template you can use for this purpose:

1. Develop a working title and subtitle.

Many authors struggle with this part, and admittedly, titles are a tricky business. One benefit of coming up with a title and subtitle early on is that they might help you put your finger on what your book is really about.

Of course, the working title should still very much capture the desired positioning. In other words, your title should serve the purpose it is intended to, even if the wording gets tweaked later on. It should reflect the spirit of your book and the precise messaging you wish to convey to your audience. For ideas, I recommend checking out books whose subject matter is similar to yours and brainstorming variations from there.

If you can't think of one now, don't stress over it. Your title doesn't need to be finalized until you start the cover design for your book. And, often times, a great title emerges from the first draft of your manuscript. For now, feel free to leave it as [WORKING TITLE.]

2. CREATE YOUR TABLE OF CONTENTS.

INTRODUCTION
At this point, there is no need to put anything here. We'll deal with the opening content during the intermediate outline stage. For now, just leave [INTRODUCTION] as a placeholder.

[INSERT A CHAPTER TITLE]
This is a one-paragraph summary containing the gist of the chapter. It should include main concepts and enough information to see how the chapter works in relation to other chapters.

[INSERT A CHAPTER TITLE]
Continue this format, as necessary, to complete the structure of your book.

CONCLUSION
Like the introduction, at this point, there is no need to flesh out your conclusion. That comes later. For now, just leave [CONCLUSION] as a placeholder.

EXPERT TIP: Establish a consistency to your chapter titles right away, even down to the level of grammar. For example, you could make all the chapter titles an *-ing* verb followed by a direct object (e.g. Ch. 1: *Changing Your Life*, Ch. 2: *Telling Your Story*, Ch. 3: *Overcoming Resistance*.) By cleaning up your chapter titles and making them short and precise, tidy and symmetrical, you will be in better shape, almost on a subconscious level, to think about everything that needs to go into your skeleton outline.

3. DETERMINE IF ANY PARTS OF YOUR BOOK REQUIRE RESEARCH.

If there is an apparent need for research, you must identify what it is and where it belongs in the outline. This means marking any places that require further development and adding explanatory notes for yourself, describing what you think is necessary.

To GIVE you an example of what a skeleton outline should look like, here is the one I made for CREATE:

WORKING TITLE: CREATE
Why did I choose this title? That one word encompasses the whole idea behind the book. Writing a book is not just an act of writing, it's an act of creation. It provides a means of transforming things that are abstract and immaterial (e.g. thoughts, ideas, stories) into something you can hold in your hands.

WORKING SUBTITLE: *A Simple Framework for Crafting Stories That Captivate, Persuade, and Inspire*
I chose this subtitle for a few reasons. First, it tells readers what benefits they can expect from the book, in a simple and direct

manner. Second, it appeals to a specific audience. And finally, it does a good job of sparking people's curiosity without giving too much away.

TABLE OF CONTENTS

[INTRODUCTION]

CHANGE YOUR LIFE…WITH A BOOK
Most people have no idea how much writing a book can change the course of their lives. From moments of catharsis to creating a legacy, this chapter explores the primary benefits of writing and publishing. It also shows readers how a book can help them attain the life they've been waiting for.

TELL YOUR STORY EFFECTIVELY
This chapter shows how to take an existing idea and make it your own by weaving personal experiences and insights into the bigger picture. It explores the importance of storytelling and discusses how to use it to create real impact on the lives of readers.

OVERCOME THE DESIRE TO PROCRASTINATE
This chapter is about overcoming any mental obstacles that the reader might face prior to starting the book creation process. It also discusses why these stumbling blocks may be present to begin with. I share my personal strategies for conquering procrastination and challenge readers to work through theirs using the 100-day journey.

POSITION YOURSELF FOR SUCCESS
This chapter helps readers decide whether a book idea is worth pursuing or not. It asks questions that identify the best audience for the book, based on the goals the reader wants to achieve. Readers are invited to think about the problem that their book will solve and the solution that they will offer. Positioning is the most

critical part of the writing process. Without it, authors are setting themselves up to fail.

DRAFT A TIME-SAVING OUTLINE
The book outline is where all the heavy lifting happens. The best way to do this is in steps, starting with a skeleton that will later be developed into a complete framework.

WRITE THE DAMN THING
Following the outline, creating the first draft should be both straightforward and efficient. This chapter discusses best practices for using the outline to "write" each chapter and provides readers with useful resources for finishing their entire book within a few days.

EDIT LIKE A BESTSELLER
Now that readers have a rough draft of their book, this chapter explains the most efficient way to edit and outsource to a second pair of trained eyes. It also stresses the importance of taking time off between writing and editing, both for one's own sanity and for the good of the book.

CREATE YOUR LEGACY
With so much information, it can be easy to feel overwhelmed, which is why this chapter ties everything together with a few notes of encouragement—reminding readers to enjoy the writing process and offering advice for seeing the endeavor through to the end.

[CONCLUSION]

Remember, your skeleton outline doesn't have to be perfect, nor should you expect it to be. It represents your first attempt at organizing your thoughts and connecting the dots in your story. Give it your best shot, take a break for a few days, then come back to it. After a second run-through, move on to the intermediate outline. You can work out the kinks there.

The Intermediate Outline

Now that you have your skeleton outline, it's time to start filling in some of the gaps. To do this, go through each chapter and answer the following questions, under your summary paragraphs:

- What is the point this chapter is trying make?
- Why does it matter?
- How does it fit in with the rest of the book?
- What other information needs to be in the chapter? (Stories, statistics, etc.)

Highlight any places where more content is needed. As you develop the intermediate outline, you will see where your material is thin, what areas require further explanation, and where examples, stories, or other data are needed. Mark these areas so that you can return to them later on.

> EXPERT TIP: It's important to format your intermediate outline as question-based, rather than answer-based, because your outline will be your guide for generating the content of your book. Think of it this way: The outline has a very specific task, which is to provide the right structure to entice you, the author, to completely layout and detail your subject matter.

The next step of the process is where you will either interview yourself or have someone else interview you against this outline. That means that you will need to talk...*a lot*. In fact, your goal should be to collect at least twice as many words in the transcript as will be in the finished book.

The worst scenario is when you don't have enough material to work with, which usually happens because the outline either doesn't contain enough detail, or it contains too much. If you don't have sufficient notes in the outline to prompt yourself to say everything you want to say, then there won't be enough content for your book.

On the other hand, if you have too many notes, you'll find yourself reading the answers to your questions off of the outline itself, rather than talking about them in great detail. It's a delicate balance, and to maintain that balance, it's best to structure your outline as open-ended questions.

Here is a basic template that you can fill out for your intermediate framework, but feel free to use whatever structure works best for you. There is no "one size fits all" here.

[RETAIN SUMMARY PARAGRAPH FROM SKELETON OUTLINE]

[INSERT POINT 1] *(Convert this to a question.)*

- [INSERT SUB-POINT 1]

    [*OPTIONAL:* INSERT SUPPORT / STORY]

- [INSERT SUB-POINT 2]

    [*OPTIONAL:* INSERT SUPPORT / STORY]

[INSERT POINT 2] *(Convert this to a question.)*

- [INSERT SUB-POINT 1]

    [*OPTIONAL:* INSERT SUPPORT / STORY]

- [INSERT SUB-POINT 2]

[*OPTIONAL:* INSERT SUPPORT / STORY]

[REPEAT AS NECESSARY]

Like chapter titles, each chapter must unfold in a consistent manner. For example, you may choose to begin each one with a story from your life and then segue into a lesson that can be drawn from that. Or you may decide to start with your arguments, then tell stories to demonstrate their application in real life. Whatever you choose, it should be the same pattern for all chapters going forward.

For reference, here is a sample outline for CHAPTER TWO of CREATE. The questions that I used to interview myself are *italicized* and the notes that summarize my responses are in ROMAN TEXT. Any areas that need further development have been **bolded**. Note how this creates a conversational structure:

Chapter 2 - Telling Your Story

This chapter is meant to expand on a previous point on how to take a pre-existing idea and make it your own by weaving personal experience and insights into the bigger picture. It will examine the importance of storytelling and apply it to creating a real impact on readers' lives. Guidelines for building a strong narrative will be provided as well as how to apply these principles to both books and business.

A. *Why is it important to tell your story?*
  1. Storytelling activates the human spirit
  2. *What does it mean to tell your story?*
     a. It's not just about creating that emotional connection with the reader
     b. It's about people understanding your "why"
     c. That's how people choose whether or not to reach out to you
     d. Your story is your unique serving proposition
  3. Lisa Nichols example
     a. Shared her story on *Oprah* and it resonated with so many people that close 10,000 reached out and she went from barely making ends meet to making over $400k in 3 months
     b. How did this happen?
        - She used Dip Theory
        - I'll explain how to do this shortly

B. How can you use it to create a big impact on the reader?
 1. Guidelines for making a great story
    a. **Be willing to take risk**
    b. Show the reader, don't tell them
       - Example of a "tell me" story
       - Example of a "show me" story
    c. Use Dip Theory
       - Letter "V" analogy
       - Apply it to every point you want to demonstrate in your book
       - Example of a good "V": Tony Robbins, Elon Musk
       - Takeaways
         - Dips are how people connect with you
         - That's how they remember the lessons you are trying to teach
    d. Be authentic
       - Your story has to cost you something
       - **Example**
    e. Effective keywords to use: "Even though I…"
       - Why it's effective
       - **Example**

 2. Applying these principles to writing your book
    a. Unpack what you were thinking, what you were feeling in your experiences
    b. Take the reader inside your vulnerability, make them feel like they are there with you
    c. This increases reader loyalty and retention
 3. Applying these principles to marketing your business
    a. Every road that leads to your market should have a story in it
    b. Your readers have other options
    c. They will choose you over only if they resonate with your story
    d. Establish that connection
    e. It all leads back to what value you're bringing your audience
C. What can you take away from all of this?
 1. Your story is the glue that sticks all of your content together
 2. Your dip is relevant because it picks up every prospective audience that you want to reach
 3. Stories are the very thing that define your unique serving proposition
 4. Weave stories into your lessons and it will take your book to the next level

As you can see, the outline is not grammatically perfect, but it gets the job done. Also worth noting is that this example is more built out than a typical intermediate outline would be. However, it gives you a better idea of how everything will lay out. Just like with the skeleton, give the intermediate outline your best shot, take a break for a few days, then come back to it. After a second run-through, move on.

TIME TO BRING your outline to 100 percent completion (or close to it.) Before you continue, look over what you've done so far. How does everything feel to you? If any hesitation or concern comes up, dig in and pinpoint the places that don't feel right. It's essential that you do this in order to verify that the book you've outlined so far represents what you want. If it doesn't, save yourself some time and make the necessary changes before you build it out any further.

At this point, our primary objective is to gather any remaining stories or examples necessary to finish the outline. To do this, make sure that you are set on the basic structure of your book. Then, go through each chapter and dig into those areas you previously marked. Always come back to the same fundamental questions:

- Does this [CHAPTER/SUB-POINT] say what you want it to say?
- Does it say it in a way that makes sense to you?
- What is the [CHAPTER/SUB-POINT] missing?
- Are the examples and anecdotes the right ones?
- Is there any material that does not belong here?

Outside of that, make sure the stories that you have included are specific and highly relevant. They should tie back to the points you've made. If you have trouble thinking of particular anecdotes, try jogging your memory with questions like *when did you first do* [INSERT TOPIC]? *What happened as a result? What is the most scared or happy you ever felt doing* [INSERT TOPIC]?

Once you feel confident in the outline of your book's chapters, it's time to clean everything up and put on the finishing touches:

INSERT QUESTIONS + STORY PROMPTS

Having your sub-points filled in makes choosing the right

questions and stories a lot easier. Ask yourself, *what do I need to ask and answer to prove the point that I'm trying to make?* Often, these questions are focused on *why is this true?* Or *why is this important?* Also, include any questions necessary to pull relevant details.

Adding in stories is more straightforward. Use the syntax STORY: [INSERT PROMPT] to indicate the appropriate place for one. Be sure your prompts are complete enough that you will remember them in a few weeks when you go to write your book. An example of a bad prompt would be FEDEX STORY, whereas a better prompt would be, *FedEx story / Bob shipped a turtle by accident, cost us a client, no attention to detail.*

STRIP EXCESSIVE LANGUAGE

After you have written the full outline and added the prompt questions, go through all of the sub-points and strip them down. You want just enough content to remind yourself what to discuss, but not enough to constitute an answer.

ADD THE INTRODUCTION

Most authors think the point of the introduction is to summarize everything they will talk about in the book, but this is a common misconception. The actual goal of a proper introduction is to engage readers and make them want to read your book. It's like an exciting sales pitch rather than an informational piece, though it does serve both purposes.

The good news here is that your introduction ties in well with your answers to the positioning questions from CHAPTER FOUR. To integrate them, follow these four simple steps:

Step One: Hook the reader. (Tell them what's interesting about your book.) The very first sentence should capture the reader's attention. This means beginning the introduction with a hook line, even if the reader doesn't understand how the line is relevant to the rest of the book. This technique is called IN MEDIAS RES, meaning, "in the middle of things," and it is very effective. For example, James Altucher's opening line to his book CHOOSE YOURSELF is "I was going to die."

If no single line jumps out at you, think about a sentence or fact in your book that makes people sit up and take notice. Or pinpoint something that will shock or interest your readers. Your hook does not have to be a killer first sentence, however. It can also be a short story, example, statistic, historical context, or even a quote.

In any case, while it's essential to have a strong and intriguing hook, it is also important that the rest of the page does the same thing. Starting out with an attention-grabbing first line and opening story will engage the reader, compel them to read more, and help lead into the rest of your material.

If you are still struggling with this, go back and review the concept of DIP THEORY discussed in CHAPTER TWO, as this is an excellent approach to capture your readers' attention and instantly build an emotional connection with them.

Step Two: Describe the reader's pain and pleasure. (Orient this person to your book's benefit.) Once you have their attention with the hook, the introduction should then answer the big question on every reader's mind: *Why should I care?* This is not about giving them simple information, nor is it not enough to list facts and figures. No one pays attention to those. People care more for stories, especially if they resonate with their problems, pain, and conflicts.

With that in mind, your material should be personal and describe, or show, the reader the massive pain that occurs from not taking the advice or lessons in your book. Why? Because pain induces action. For example, if your book is about how to drive traffic to a site, you need to ask yourself, *what is an example of how my business suffered when we didn't have traffic flowing to our website?*

Once you've established the pain, then the orientation material should demonstrate the benefits of taking action. Show your readers what they have to look forward to and why it's worth doing. Using the same example, you could ask yourself, *what is something my business can do now because we have so much traffic coming to our website?*

Step Three: Tell your readers why they should listen to you. (Establish author authority.) Your credibility as an author must be secured early on in the book. While this is established on the ABOUT THE AUTHOR page as well as on the book's back cover (briefly), the introduction is where you do most of the legwork. To do this, ask yourself, *why am I qualified, even uniquely qualified, to write this book? Why should the reader credit what I have to say?* From there, work those answers into your content.

Step Four: Tell the readers what they will learn. (Present a clear benefit statement.) The introduction should end with a very clear-cut thesis of what the reader can expect to learn from your book. Make sure that this benefit statement is so simple and straightforward that even a seventh-grader could identify and understand it. What you are essentially saying to readers here is: *This is how you are going to do this. I'm going to walk you through it, step-by-step, until you understand exactly how it's done.*

Once you get them excited about what they're going to learn, the job of the introduction is done. Your readers will want to dive in to the rest of the content, so get out of their way and end by jumping right into the first chapter of your book.

This is a simple formula, and virtually all the best books you've ever read have an introduction that follows this exact process.

ADD THE CONCLUSION

Not all books need conclusions but almost every non-fiction book does. Conclusions serve to pull the threads of a book together, reinforce the author's message, and send readers away with a strong call to action. In other words, if your book were a package, your conclusion would be the shipping twine that ties it all up beautifully.

By definition, a conclusion is built upon the content that comes before it. It doesn't make any sense standing on its own. What this means is that the conclusion should refer back to earlier material in the book, even as far back as the introduction. As such, they are laid out according to what the author has said up to this point. Except for stories and anecdotes, none of the content in your conclusion should be new to the reader.

Generally speaking, a conclusion must do the following things (unless it is a memoir):

- Restate the thesis of the book
- Reprise or summarize key points
- Create some sort of call to action

The goal of the call to action is to inspire enthusiasm and spur readers to act, but in a way that reflects your genuine voice. It can be overt and specific or subtle and broad. Calls to action generally take on a more authoritative tone than the rest of the material. If readers were to read between the lines, they would recognize that the call to action is your way of saying, *Now that you have the tools you need, go out there and use them!*

That said, some authors are not comfortable with such a direct approach, as it can feel at odds with their well-educated manner. But a call to action doesn't have to come across in a superficial pep-rally way. It can be whatever you want it to be, whatever feels natural to you.

The flip side of this is authors who drift toward writing a book that is a glorified sales brochure. *Do not do this.* You must keep faith with the reader all the way to the end, which means delivering real value throughout your book, not just promotional marketing. Failure to do this will mean the failure of your book. While you want to get the reader excited and ready to take action, you don't want to provide hollow words of encouragement. The more specific and reflective of your distinct voice and spirit, the better.

The conclusion is also an excellent place to direct readers to specific resources. Take the opportunity to send them off in the right direction, equipped with the information they need. But, again, don't make it seem like the whole book was about pitching your company or services.

Remember that the most important currency you have is your readers' trust. At the beginning of the book, you convinced them to accept you as a guide. Don't become a salesman at the end, or you'll lose their confidence. This means delivering real value all the way through.

Readers are smart. They know that you have an interest in the subject, and they can come to their own conclusions about contacting you. If you want to ask them to get in touch, do so authentically—from a place of trying to help *them*, not yourself. Tell people you want to hear their feedback or offer help if they need it. You can even give out your email if you'd like. But if your website or the name of your company is on your ABOUT THE AUTHOR page, that is more than sufficient.

Ultimately, your goal is to lead readers to respect and admire you and your work and to choose to contact you because they have sold themselves, not because you sold them.

Other Things Your Conclusion Must Not Do:

- Introduce new concepts, sources or ideas
- Be out of alignment with the content or message of your book
- Be more than a few pages (2,000 words, *at most*)

Critical Questions for Shaping Your Conclusion:

- Specifically, what do you want readers to remember from your book?

- What parting words do you want to leave with them?
- When readers tell their friends about the book, what do you want them to say?
- When they finish the last sentence and put the book down, what is the first thing you want them to do? (*This is the* CALL TO ACTION *question.*)

ADD THE ABOUT THE AUTHOR PAGE

Contrary to popular belief, the standard professional bio is not appropriate for a book. Instead, you want to build one tailored specifically to this project. With that said, here are a few fundamental questions that you can add to your outline, after the conclusion:

- What do you want to say on your ABOUT THE AUTHOR page?
- What do you want to say about your work?
- What about your qualifications?
- Do you want to include anything about your family or where you live?
- Do you want to provide your website or contact info?
- Would you like this to have a light or humorous tone?

Again, as with the skeleton and the intermediate outlines, once you're done, take a break for a few days and then come back to it. After reviewing it once or twice, it's time to lock it in.

LOCK IN YOUR OUTLINE

AT THIS POINT, you've most likely read through and reflected on your outline a handful of times. And while you may be eager to move on from this tedious process, it is crucial that you make sure that your outline feels right to you. That said, there is no rush here. If you want to make any minor changes, go ahead. Root out any possible problems or objections and take the time to solve them now.

In the end, your outline should contain just enough information that you can imagine yourself talking through your book, using this framework as a guide. Ask yourself, *am I comfortable with how everything lays out? Can I see myself using this outline as a guide for an interview about these ideas? Is this the book I want to write?*

If the answer to those questions is YES, then go ahead and lock it in. If the answer is NO, that's okay too. Take the extra time you need to get your outline exactly how you want it.

CONGRATULATIONS! The hardest part is over (*seriously.*) With all that heavy lifting done, you can now move on to writing your book.

SIX

Write the Damn Thing

"ABRACADABRA *comes from the Aramaic phrase* AVRA KEHDABRA *which means, literally,* I WILL CREATE AS I SPEAK." - Unknown

---

FINALLY! We have arrived at the most anticipated part of the step of the process: *actually writing your book*! This is where you get to take all of your stories and insights and put them into the first draft.

Unlike most authors, the one issue that you will not encounter here is that of the BLANK PAGE PROBLEM. If you haven't heard of this quagmire before, all you need to know is that it happens to writers who haven't taken the time to structure their thoughts into an outline. When they go to write, they end up staring at a blank white screen, day after day, not making any progress at all. But because you've done all of the hard work upfront, you have nothing to worry about here.

At this point, a lot of people dread the thought of having to sit down and write their book. This is because writing is uncomfortable and foreign territory for many people. However, speaking in a conversational manner is not. In fact, most people enjoy talking, especially when it comes to sharing their ideas with others. This is why we are going to "write" your book using voice dictation.

If you constructed your outline correctly, it should be filled with the questions you need to get your ideas out of your head and down onto paper. Now, it is time is record yourself answering these questions. Or, if you'd like, have a friend interview you instead. A lot of professionals who use this method prefer the latter because it forces them to elaborate and explain their thought processes more thoroughly. It is also easier to talk when someone else is present because it creates a more casual, conversational tone, which ultimately leads to a better book.

If, however, you have to interview yourself, like I often do, follow the outline and picture a specific person in your head. Imagine that the avatar you created in your positioning is sitting in front of you and talk to him (or her.) Sure, you might feel a bit awkward at first, but you'll get used to it. As for the interview itself, keep the following guidelines in mind:

THE GOLDEN RULE: *Stick to your outline.* Doing so will make editing later on more comfortable and less frustrating.

USE BEGINNER'S MIND. To make sure you explain everything in its entirety, take on the mindset of an eight-year-old. This means asking the question *"why?"* as often as possible. Go deep here and take your time.

PUT YOURSELF IN THE READERS' SHOES. Think about what they would want to know, clarify, and understand. If someone else is interviewing you, tell him that he represents the reader. If he is confused at all, the reader will be too, so make sure that he asks if he needs anything clarified.

KEEP THINGS COMFORTABLE AND CONVERSATIONAL. It's okay if you find yourself repeating certain things; just be sure to cover each question thoroughly. You can always cut out the redundant parts later on. Open up and do not hold back.

IF YOU ARE HAVING SOMEONE ELSE INTERVIEW YOU, be sure to tell him beforehand not to interrupt your flow of thoughts. If he has questions, or needs further clarification on anything, have him wait until you finish speaking. Also, remind him that he should never add his own thoughts to your subject matter. This is, after all, *your* book, not his.

TO AVOID BEING TOO VAGUE, use specific stories or events that demonstrate your main points. If you need help with this, some good prompts are:

- *Talk about a day when...*
- *Talk about the time when...*
- *Tell the story of...*
- *Give me an example of a time that you* [INSERT ACTIVITY] *that didn't work?*
- *What day did you decide to* [INSERT ACTIVITY]*? What happened?*

WHENEVER YOU PROVIDE AN EXAMPLE OR TELL A STORY, make sure that you talk about the bigger lessons that came out of it. How does your story fit in with the rest of the book? What lessons did you learn from that specific experience?

PROVIDE SPECIFIC STEP-BY-STEP INSTRUCTIONS, WHEN APPROPRIATE. For instance, if you say, *I made $1 million in twelve months*, explain how you did that. Always back up your assertions with evidence.

MOST IMPORTANTLY, RECORD EVERYTHING YOU SAY! Use a voice recorder or an app to document all of your interviews, as these recordings will later be transcribed to form the first draft of your manuscript. There are plenty of free ones that can be found through the APP STORE, GOOGLE PLAY or online. *Do not forget to do this.*

Again, your job is to be both an advocate for your reader as well as the author of the story you're telling. Taking the time to explore your writing from the perspective of the reader—who knows nothing or very little about your topic—is essential because your reader isn't there to ask those questions. Doing this takes your writing to a whole new level of depth. It also gets you more content for whatever chapter you're struggling with. And having more content is always better than having less.

It's worth noting that this point in the process is typically when most writers become overcritical and hard on themselves. Sooner or later, they grow frustrated and even a little discouraged, eventually spending more and more time away from the book before putting it aside and turning their attention to something else entirely.

This happens more often than you think. Writers sit down with their laptops and freshly brewed coffee, often in the early hours of the morning, and eagerly begin typing away. Meanwhile, they dream of one day being able to boast about the release of their next book.

Of course, everything seems to go smoothly at first: Motivation is top-notch. Productivity is relatively high. And every day they are able to quantify their progress, excited as they get closer to that final stretch.

But sooner or later they hit a wall. They get stuck somewhere in the process of word-smithing and inevitably find themselves in a state of crisis: *Why did we choose to become writers? What if no one likes what we have to say? What if these ideas and stories aren't good enough?*

If you find yourself in a similar state, it's important to remember that, just like with any new hobby, the trick to sticking with it is to let your inner beginner live alongside your inner expert. The beginner may be an idiot, but she knows how to have fun. And if you don't let her play with you anymore, you risk things becoming rather dull and uninspired.

Why is this important? Because readers can *feel* the excitement and energy that you put into each page and every chapter. If you're not excited or passionate about what you're doing or what you're writing about, they won't be either. So, relax, take your time, and try to have some fun! And if it makes the job more pleasant, break things up by adding a few days of downtime between chapters.

AFTER YOU'VE FINISHED with the interviews, there are one of three approaches you can take:

1. Have each recording transcribed. Then rewrite the transcribed document, paragraph-by-paragraph, before moving on to the next chapter.
2. Or, listen to each audio recording and transcribe it yourself, working through the coherency as you go along.
3. Alternatively, take the path of least resistance and use DRAGON to transcribe your recordings as you speak, then rework specific paragraphs for clarity and fluidity.

I find that the last approach makes the rewriting process more comfortable to work through. It also makes the editing process less daunting. Not only does DRAGON give me complete control over the timeline of my book, it also means that I don't have to rely on someone else to get the job done. But, as always, you should do what works best for you. I know a lot of people who want to get through the recordings before they even consider rewrites. That approach makes a lot of sense, because it allows you stay focused on one thing before moving on to the next. But as a more experienced writer, I like to blend voice dictation and rewrites for my own sanity. That said, here are a few other tips that can help you with the writing process:

SERIOUSLY, TAKE ADVANTAGE OF VOICE DICTATION!

Over the past few years, I have developed a love-hate relationship with this approach. When I first discovered it, I thought it would be a total game-changer. But to my disappointment, I found that most apps and dictation software were not as accurate as I thought they would be, which meant that I spent way too much time trying to fix whatever the software spit out. It was a complete pain-in-the-ass, and I wouldn't wish that kind of agony on anyone, not even my worst enemies. I wasn't overly thrilled by the idea of outsourcing these transcriptions either because I felt like it left too much room for human error. But what is a girl to do?

That's when I found Chris Fox's book, 5000 WORDS PER HOUR. He had a similar experience with voice dictation until he discovered the machine learning software I previously mentioned. *This time it really was a game-changer.*

Think about it: The average person speaks between 142 and 160 words per minute. The average typing speed is about 40 to 44 words per minute. Even if you speak slowly, at about 80 words per minute, assuming that your book falls within the average nonfiction length range of 20,000 to 30,000 words, it would only take six to seven hours to write your entire book with this software!

Granted, it can take some time to get comfortable with voice dictation, and doesn't always come out perfect. But this approach is highly efficient and can save you *a lot* of time. (Time that could be spent doing other things.) I will leave a link for DRAGON in the RESOURCES section if you are interested in learning more.

TRY EXPERIMENTING WITH WRITING SPRINTS.

I first heard about writing sprints from Chris Fox. These are predefined lengths of time where you do nothing but write. Or, in this case, dictate. Writing sprints always have a clearly defined start and end time, and during this window, you do nothing else.

No web surfing.
No answering the phone.
No checking emails or texts.
No eating food.

All of those things should be handled before or after. What you will find when doing writing sprints is that your chapters come together much faster. But this only happens if you do not stop until you are finished with the time interval that you have set aside for yourself. *Do not pause.* Just keep writing until your timer goes off.

The purpose of this exercise is to get you into flow state, where your brain naturally focuses on an activity—in this case, writing your book—to the exclusion of all else. The words flow out onto the page, whole chapters burst out of you, and you end up shocked by the rapid progress that you've made on your book. In fact, writing sprints tie-in well with the 100-DAY JOURNEY I described in CHAPTER THREE. That being said, here's how I do mine:

Step One: Open my word processor of choice to a blank document. (I prefer SCRIVENER.)

Step Two: Turn off the Wi-Fi on my computer and put my phone either in airplane mode or on Do Not Disturb.

Step Three: Pull up the outline for whatever chapter I want to work on.

Step Four: Launch my DRAGON dictation software.

Step Five: Set my timer for thirty minutes and begin interviewing myself, using the outline as a guide.

EXPERT TIP: Give yourself permission to suck. What I mean by that is, once you start writing (or dictating), you are not allowed to tinker with or edit it at all. This means *no stopping* and *no going back*, not even to correct typos created by the software.

Don't worry, you'll have a chance to rewrite all the paragraphs that sound "off" and clean up your writing later when you come back to edit. For now, stay focused on recording your ideas and stories. Again, nothing needs to be perfect. In fact, it won't be. The point here is to get through every chapter and finish your book before you go back and start picking it apart.

ADAPT SECTIONS OR CHAPTERS INTO MEDIUM ARTICLES, THEN POST.

In CHAPTER THREE, I talked about how I used the MEDIUM platform to beat procrastination and finish my book. But not everyone will feel comfortable with this approach, and I respect that. The only reasons you may want to consider it are:

1. Publishing online forces you to confront the fear of sharing your thoughts with others before the book is published.
2. It holds you accountable to an audience. Platform users expect you to publish content consistently and frequently—an expectation that can help you write your book much faster.
3. Posting online helps you build up a loyal fan base that's interested in learning more about your book before it hits the market.
4. You can also use the early reader engagement to collect emails for sending updates about the book's release.
5. Online publication means that you need to check the

clarity of your writing in advance, making it less tedious to edit the full book later on.

That said, you should *not* publish your chapters online to get feedback from your peers. Sure, people might offer suggestions or ask for clarification on certain sub-points that you may have otherwise missed. However, the only people whose feedback you should be interested in is your primary audience. Outside of that, take all suggestions with a grain of salt, including those from family and close friends.

A WORD OF CAUTION: You won't be able to enroll your book in KINDLE SELECT or KINDLE UNLIMITED if more than ten percent of it is available elsewhere online. So, use your own discretion here.

Once you've made it through your entire outline, it's time to get organized. Remember that the structure is there, even if it's a bit difficult to see.

To organize all of my materials, I like to use SCRIVENER. It's quite affordable, but if you don't want to spend any money, an alternative would be to separate each chapter into its own WORD file or GOOGLE document. Doing this will make things less overwhelming going forward. Once you've created a separate file for each chapter:

1. Label each document with the chapter title.
2. Copy and paste the outline sections for every chapter at the top of each document.
3. Then copy and paste the entire audio transcript for each chapter below its respective outline.

Now it's time for the rewrite. The most effective way to do this is to first read through the outline for the chapter you are working on to remind yourself of the key points you wanted to make. Then read through the transcript for that chapter and recall *how* you made all of your points. After that, go through, paragraph-by-paragraph, and rewrite each one. If you find that something isn't worth keeping, go ahead and cut it out.

Once you have done this for all paragraphs, do a quick read-through of the chapter to make sure that the flow of ideas makes sense and that the concepts are well-explained. Don't worry about getting everything perfect. (That is what editing is for.) Right now, just focus on establishing the clarity and fluidity of your book.

After all of this is done, you will have the first draft of your manuscript in your hands. And that calls for a major celebration! Pat yourself on the back and take a week or two off before moving on to editing, so that you can feel refreshed for the final step of the creation process.

Seriously, take a break. You've earned it! Go out and celebrate this massive accomplishment. And know that you have done what most people will never do in their lifetimes: *You have written a book and created your legacy in doing so.*

SEVEN

Edit Like a Bestseller

"Editing might be a bloody trade, but knives aren't the exclusive property of butchers. Surgeons use them too." - Blake Morrison

It took five days and a little over 33,000 words to write this book. I'm not saying that to brag or to show off. I'm doing it because I want to take you behind the scenes of my life during that window of time and explain the events that followed.

The week I wrote CREATE consisted of 19-hour work days, severe sleep deprivation, a complete lack of self-care, and total isolation. During this time, my body expressed its contempt for the hell I was putting it through in every way imaginable, which meant that I gained a few pounds, broke out into a random case of hives, and even went through a mild depression. There were also moments when I wondered what the hell I was thinking when I decided to do this to myself *(although I never found a reasonable answer.)*

> NOTE: To those of you reading this, I do not recommend taking this approach.

You would think that when I finished my book, my mind would calm down and I would go celebrate, *but I didn't*. Instead, I had built up so much energy and excitement that the only thing I wanted to do was jump right into editing. *Big mistake.*

I don't know whether I couldn't take a break because of a desperate need to share this collection of thoughts and experiences with future readers, or whether it was the fear that I would never return to finish what I started if I did. Who knows? Maybe I'm just a workaholic. But what followed was nothing less than sheer exhaustion and burnout, along with a severe bout of the flu. *This is why I would like to emphasize the importance of taking time off between writing and editing your book.*

Coincidentally, about three days after I completed the first draft, I had booked a flight to the USA to visit my family. (I was living in Iceland at the time.) It was the perfect opportunity to put my manuscript aside and enjoy being home. *Instead,* I decided to push myself a little further and use the five-hour flight to start chipping away at edits. *I'll stop working as soon as we land,* I told myself.

Halfway through the flight, however, my brain decided to switch off and force me into recovery mode...*for the next ten days.* One can imagine my irritation at not being able to work anymore. But in hindsight, I see how vital and necessary that time-out was to gain a fresh perspective on my book.

What my brain was trying to tell my stubborn ego was that it needed some time to process what I had just done. And when I returned to work on the book two weeks later, I found dozens of mistakes that I had missed before.

By jumping straight into the editing phase, my mind was so exhausted that it skipped over awkward phrases and other areas that felt "off." However, after I had time to clear my mind, I was able to make corrections quickly and efficiently and fix the problem sections in each chapter.

The only thing my previous edits did for me was create *more work*, and they were certainly not as optimized as they would have been if I had simply walked away as soon as I finished writing the first draft. So, if you learn anything from this tale of poor judgment, it should be that a one- or two-week vacation from your manuscript makes a *significant* difference in your ability to edit. But once you've taken that vacation, it's time to move on to editing your manuscript like a bestselling author.

It's important to note that editing is not just about correcting grammar and checking for typos. In fact, there are four stages of edits to work through:

The first stage is content editing. This is the most brutal and heartbreaking part of the process. Be prepared to rip your book apart and put it back together again, this time making it better.

The second stage is line editing. This is about making sure that every sentence and paragraph are as good as they can be. Imagine that a national newspaper has asked to quote a passage from your book. The question you have to ask yourself is, *would I be happy with any line or paragraph they use?* Reading every sentence, paragraph, and chapter out loud is the acid test. If it makes you cringe, rewrite it.

The third stage is copy editing. This is about correcting grammatical errors. It's making sure that your tone is consistent and that your point-of-view doesn't change halfway through the book. Copy editing is *not* something that you should do on your own. Instead, hire a professional—someone who will be thorough all the way through to the end. Besides, at this point, you will be sick of going through your book with a fine-tooth comb, and you'll be more willing to overlook these kinds of errors.

THE FOURTH AND FINAL STAGE IS PROOFREADING. This involves catching any last-minute mistakes or errors that have crept into your manuscript during the edits. It's best to have someone else do this for you as well (preferably, a professional) because, at this point, it's likely that you will just see what you want to see on the page. *Note:* Proofreading should be done *after* your book has been formatted.

A WORD OF CAUTION: Don't be in a hurry to send out your manuscript, hoping someone else will fix all of this for you. The best approach is to take on the content and line edits yourself, then outsource the copy edits and proofread to a professional.

Now, let's dive into the process for tackling each of these editing passes, in detail, starting with the CONTENT EDITS. To do this, we'll implement the following two-step process used by all bestselling authors:

1. Read your manuscript out loud to yourself or to another person.
2. Then make the necessary changes.

The reason to start with reading your manuscript out loud is that it allows you to find anything that sounds strange or awkward. Your primary aim here should be to make your writing no more complicated than if you were talking about your subject matter with a good friend. Your sentences should be simple and easy to read. So, go ahead and sit down with a printout of your manuscript and begin to read through it out loud.

As you do this, ask yourself, *does this sound the same way I'd say it to someone if I were speaking with him face-to-face? Does this feel right to me?* While reading your manuscript aloud, you will inevitably hear errors and phrasings you want to fix, as well as sentences that sound a bit "off." Mark any areas you wish to rework, then move on. You don't need to make the revisions right then and there, but it's important to make note of them so that you can go back and make changes later.

After you've gone through this first round of revisions, go back and implement the changes you made. Then leave your manuscript alone for a few days to clear your head. And whatever you do, do not make the same mistake I did by obsessing over it. Put it out of sight and out of mind during your time off.

That said, even though it's important to take a break, it is just as important to set a deadline for when you will return to your manuscript. Otherwise, you risk procrastinating for months and even abandoning your endeavor altogether. This happens more often than you think. It's a delicate balance that every aspiring author must face at some point. But if you go into it with an awareness of what could happen, you will be better prepared to overcome this deadly trap and see your book through to the end.

If you've made it this far, congratulations. You are now ahead of 95 percent of writers, simply because you managed to write in the spoken language.

Now that you know your manuscript reads well, it's time to make sure that your book says exactly what you want it to say (a.k.a. LINE EDITS.) To do this, we have to get nit-picky. Start by reading through each sentence, while asking the following questions:

- What point am I trying to make in this sentence?
- Is it clear what I'm trying to say?
- Is this sentence as simple as possible without losing meaning?
- Is this sentence as short as possible without losing meaning?
- Did I leave anything out that is necessary to understand my point?

Once you have finished combing through each sentence with these questions, repeat the process for each paragraph. Once you finish combing through each paragraph, repeat this process for each chapter. Yes, the process is tedious. But the whole point is to cut out any fluff from your book, making it sound sharper and more refined. It also allows you to really drive home your main points.

NOW THAT YOU have completed the first two passes of your book, it's time to take things one step further with COPY EDITING and PROOFREADING, which is why I highly recommend using a professional. Personally, I like to use BOOK BUTCHERS or REEDSY, but there are plenty of other online marketplaces to find a strong editor.

Now I understand if you are reluctant to spend any money creating your book. However, realistically, you should expect to invest *some* financial resources in this endeavor in order to give your book the best possible chance of success. And, if I had to recommend any place to spend money, it would be on editing and cover design.

That said, while this book does not go into publishing and marketing—in order to avoid information overload—I cannot stress enough the importance of both self-editing and working with a professional on your manuscript. *Do not* leave it in the hands of a friend or family member because it can end up creating more problems for you down the road. Besides, more often than not, your friends and family are *not* the types of readers that you are targeting, so their feedback won't be very helpful.

Of course, if you *do* have access to the exact audience that you want to reach with your book, you could ask them for feedback on your manuscript. Take advantage of questions like, *what helps you most in the book? What chapters do you wish had more content? Where did you get lost or confused?* Listen to your readers' feedback but use your own ideas and knowledge to fix the problem. Remember that no one knows your book or subject matter better than you do.

Other Things to Keep in Mind as You Edit:

- In CHAPTER FIVE, I discussed the importance of the introduction in capturing your readers' attention. The same thing applies to the opening of each chapter. Keep your readers hooked as they go through your book by opening every chapter with a clear goal and benefit statement.
- Each chapter should connect to the following one. All paragraphs within a chapter should also connect. What this means is that *transitions are crucial* so pay attention to the way everything flows together. Doing so will make your book far more enjoyable to the reader.
- Last but not least, it's okay if you need to rewrite certain passages yet again. It's all part of the editing process.

AFTER SELF-EDITING and implementing the corrections made by a professional, do one last pass on your manuscript, making any last-minute changes. *Then move on.*

Remember that the whole point of writing this is to share its contents with others. If you never pass along your wisdom, then you will have wasted a lot of time and energy creating your book.

So don't let the fear of telling your story or expressing your ideas —or any other concerns surrounding your book—hold you back from publishing.

At least one person out there, and probably many more, wants to learn what you have to teach them. You have an obligation to yourself and your readers to stop editing and get your book out there, even if it isn't perfect. After all, your story can only help your audience if it's available for them to buy.

ONE LAST THING: As mentioned earlier, the specifics of publishing and marketing are beyond the scope of this book. However, I recommend checking out the RESOURCES section for tools and platforms that can help you navigate these areas.

EIGHT

Create Your Legacy

"A book is a dream that you hold in your hands." - Neil Gaiman

DURING MY TRIP home to the States, my mom reminded me of a computer I had built as a little girl.

"Do you remember when you were seven or eight years old and you wanted a computer for your birthday? Your dad and I thought you were too young, so we said that you would have to wait another year or two. Shortly after that, you made one out of paper and tape. You drew yourself a keyboard, a mouse, a screen, even a power button. And when it was finished, you carried it around the house with you. Then, you found a place to sit down, open your laptop, and start typing away. It was so cute."

"I think I remember that. The two pieces of paper refused to stay open. Eventually, I got so frustrated that I made a small stand to lean the top piece against and taped it there so it would stay."

"You were always creating things like that: paper laptops, cardboard airplanes, solar toasters made out of pizza boxes. Remember the carousel you built out of dog leashes and old rocking horses?" she asked with a laugh.

Create Your Legacy

I welcomed my mother's recollection of these things, as I had tucked away those childish aspirations and failed inventions long ago. But the more I thought about it, the more I realized how important it was for her to remind me of these moments from my childhood.

As a kid, nothing stood in my way. Not money. Not time. Not the word NO. And certainly not thoughts of being practical or realistic. In fact, I once waited an entire day to have breakfast because that solar toaster was terrible at toasting bagels.

Of course, most of my creations never worked out, but I didn't mind. All I cared about was that they were fun to create. I lost myself in these little adventures. And after each one, I experienced the kind of magic and immense satisfaction that goes along with turning an idea into something tangible and real. Creativity is always like that—it's a shame that most of us forget how powerful it is as we transition into adulthood.

Remember how, as kids, there was always this sense of, *let's just see what I can get away with?* For me it was, *let's see how high I can climb up this tree!* And *I wonder if I can sneak up on the roof and grab that frisbee before Mom catches me.* For my sisters it was, *let's give each other haircuts!* Or *let's see if Dad finds that sticky piece of gum we left in his jacket pocket.*

Yes, my sisters and I often tested the boundaries of our parents' love and patience. And yet, our intentions weren't malicious; they were meant to be playful. We knew that our parents worked hard and had to deal with the stresses of adult life. So, as children, we wanted to remind them of the importance of play and fun.

Of course, now that I'm an adult, I realize how easy it is to make a big deal out of things:

The apartment has to get clean before our parents visit.

The power bill is $30 more this month than it was last month...when did we forget to turn off the lights?

These student loans are going to take FOREVER *to pay off.*

But sooner or later, we realize that it's absurd to worry about such things because worrying doesn't change anything. It just causes us to suffer twice. Recently, this got me thinking: *Why not try taking a different approach?* Why not adopt that same childish mindset of, *let's see what I can get away with?*

I don't mean that in an illegal or unethical sense, but rather as a reminder that life is really just a game and should be treated as such. Sure, we all face more responsibility and pressure as adults than as children, but that hasn't stopped other people, has it? You know, the ones who decided to pursue their BIG DREAMS and kick ass along the way?

Personally, I like to think that part of the reason successful people achieve what they set out to do is because they play these games of, *let's see what we can get away with.*

Have you ever wondered what would happen if you said to yourself: *Let's see if I can get away with starting my own successful business?*

I'm curious if I can lose fifty pounds before my next birthday.

Let's see if I can make a six-figure income this year.

I wonder if I can write my book and publish it in the next six months.

What would happen if you took some pressure off your adult self and jumped back into an exciting creative pursuit like penning the next *New York Times* bestseller?

The point here is that each of us can choose the world we want to live in, but that reality is entirely a matter of perspective. In other words, when we decide to create the reality we want to experience, life happens as we choose.

Until now, you have likely been controlled and shaped by the world around you. Life has always happened *to you*. But now, you have the opportunity to use the unique perspectives that came out of everything you have ever lived through to teach others and *create* a life of your choosing.

When you connect with the world that lives *inside* of you, which holds everything you need to write your book, you will realize that you have the power to change the world *outside* of you too. And, in doing so, you can breathe life into your vision of the future and into any dreams that you may have set aside years ago.

By telling your story and sharing your ideas through the written word, you have an opportunity to contribute to the growth of other human beings. This is your chance to become a thought leader, and to use your unique insight and experience to create a better world—both for yourself and for others.

Whatever has happened in your life, including your greatest heartache and disappointment, is exactly what was needed to help you reach the next level of personal growth and evolution. Each of these human experiences, big or small, happened to you, so that one day you could use them in service to others. For years, they have been nudging you toward what you were always meant to do.

But this kind of clarity has to come from within. To achieve the extraordinary results you want out of life, it's important that you create your own special instructions. It starts by asking, *what is the one thing I can do to make everything surrounding my* BIG DREAM *easier?*

Is it helping others find you so that they can work with you?

Is it launching a new career?

Is it publishing a bestseller?

Asking this question is the first step in getting to where you want to go. It serves as both a roadmap for the bigger picture and a compass for your next steps. Because the extraordinary results we seek from life are seldom coincidental. Rather, they come out of every decision we make and from the corresponding measures we take. This is why the formula for achieving extraordinary results—and for creating a life of your choosing—is knowing what matters to you and taking daily doses of action that are in alignment with what you seek.

When we have specific goals for our lives, clarity comes faster. This, in turn, leads to more conviction in our direction, which usually leads to faster decisions. By making faster decisions, we end up with better choices. And, better choices give us the opportunity to have extraordinary experiences. Therefore, knowing where you are going helps you achieve the greatest possible results and experiences that life (and your book) have to offer.

That said, I recognize that the idea of writing a book can be a little intimidating at first, which is why I would like to leave you with one last story. And I hope you will find it as encouraging as I did.

SOMEONE ONCE GAVE me a formula to lead a more purposeful life, and it went something like this:

In order to live a life that is worthy of you, in both meaning and fulfillment, you have to focus on, and be aware of, what excites you most. Then, do what excites you to the best of your abilities. But, above all, do so without any expectations.

After hearing this, I began to regularly check in with myself to get a sense for what excited me the most. I did this by asking, *does this activity feel authentic? Does it feel good? Does it feel like me?*

Of course, the activity that resonated the most was the act of writing. And what I've always loved about writing is how quickly it allows me to immerse myself in my imagination. It's a feeling like no other—a feeling of energetic focus, of pure enjoyment in the process, of losing all sense of time for hours on end. There was only one other time in my life where I experienced something like this, and that was as a child, building those cardboard airplanes and makeshift laptops.

As I grew older, writing became more and more important to me, serving as a mini hiatus from the demands of everyday life. To this day, it makes me feel both alive and grateful. After all, most people exist in one world and see things from a single perspective. But as a writer, I am lucky enough to create many worlds and experience them through the eyes of many characters.

Of course, the older I got, the less time I found for writing. It became less and less of a priority as I let other things get in the way—like my nine-to-five job, paying the bills, spending time with friends, traveling. And after a few years, the lack of creativity in my life began to eat away at me. It was only when I decided to prioritize writing again that I remembered how cathartic the creative process can be.

I've often heard that stories inspire change because they give us hope. They show us that things can get better—not only for those who read stories but also for those who write them. Personally, I could not agree more.

Over the years, writing has made me aware of where and when I use my comfort zone to limit my true potential. It has also shown me the world of possibilities that exist for writers. But, in order to access these possibilities, one has to surrender to the creative process rather than resist it.

Not to say that writing doesn't have its limitations; it does. In fact, as I was writing this book, I heard an annoying little voice in my head that liked to pester me with questions like:

Wait, how will publishing a book do anything meaningful for your life?

What can writing possibly do to make things better for you?

Sure, you enjoy writing, but that doesn't mean it can support you.

This is crazy! You are crazy!

As you can imagine, this eventually created a minor internal crisis. However much I tried to ignore it, this voice knew its way around my thoughts. She understood which insecurities she could use to sow self-doubt in what I was doing and create uncertainty about the path that lay ahead. But I soon realized that this voice was actually the sound of expectation—expectations that were standing in the way of my BIG DREAM.

Fortunately, around this time, I came across a story about a woman who had gone through something similar on her own journey. The woman was an attorney who had an interest in past lives. She was so intrigued by them, in fact, that she took a workshop on past life regressions run by Brian Weiss. Shortly after that, she received the following email:

WE ARE REACHING OUT TO EVERYONE WHO HAS EVER STUDIED WITH US OR COME TO OUR WORKSHOPS. PLEASE SEND US YOUR REGRESSION STORIES—EITHER PERSONAL OR THOSE OF YOUR CLIENTS—BECAUSE WE ARE WRITING A BOOK AND WE WANT TO INCLUDE YOUR STORIES IN IT.

When the attorney read this email, she was excited for the book's release. However, regarding their request for submissions, she couldn't help but think, *if I send in my own stories, what's in it for me?* She didn't see how contributing to this book would add any value to her life. She only thought about how it would benefit the company and their book sales. After all, they were the ones getting published and receiving the royalties. But after further contemplation, the attorney decided to go ahead and do it for kicks and giggles.

What ultimately convinced her was a little voice that said, *Mira, you love talking about past life regression. You would do it for free. This is an exciting thing for you. Just send them some stories.* So, she sat down and wrote a few out.

When Mira immersed herself in her project, she felt overwhelmed by excitement and happiness. Here she was, writing about something she truly loved; something that meant a lot to her.

By the time she finished, she decided to submit the stories

using her real name. This, of course, was very nerve racking, considering that she worked in a conservative legal environment. Mira was afraid that if word got out about her interest in past lives, it would jeopardize her career because people would no longer take her seriously. This caused her to have a moment of panic: *What did I just do? Maybe I should follow-up and ask them to edit my name out?* But in the end, she decided to let it go.

Sometime after that, Mira received the following email:

WE LOVED YOUR STORIES. AND EVEN THOUGH WE RECEIVED 400 SUBMISSIONS FOR THIS BOOK, WE PICKED ALL THREE OF YOURS BECAUSE THEY WERE SO WELL-WRITTEN. THEY EXEMPLIFIED POINTS THAT ARE IMPORTANT TO MAKE, AND THEY HAVE MANY GOOD LESSONS TO TEACH. SO, CONGRATULATIONS! YOU ARE GOING TO BE INCLUDED IN OUR BOOK!

More time passed before she heard anything else. Then, one day, she woke up to find this in her inbox:

MIRA, WE ARE GOING TO BE ON OPRAH SUPER SOUL SUNDAY. AS PART OF PROMOTING THE BOOK, THE PRODUCERS OF THE SHOW WENT THROUGH THE WHOLE THING. AND OUT OF ALL THE STORIES, THEY PICKED THE ONE OF HOW YOU STARTED DOING PAST LIFE REGRESSION. WE JUST WANTED TO LET YOU KNOW THAT YOUR STORY IS ALREADY ON OPRAH'S WEBSITE AND HAS BEEN USED FOR THE PROMOTION.

Her immediate response? *Oh My God. This is it.*

When she first felt that inspirational nudge to write these stories, Mira could not have foreseen how everything would play out. Nor could she have known that these stories would eventually be promoted by Oprah and her people. Yet, she would never have experienced any of this if she had allowed her expectations to get in the way of what she wanted to do. It only happened because she followed that moment of, *this feels good and exciting. This is totally who I am.*

After reading Mira's story, I decided it was time to finish what I had started and to pursue my love of writing without any expectation of where it would lead me.

Sure, it would have been easy to give in to that inner voice of doubt and insecurity. It would have been *even easier* to accept that traditional publishing was the only way for others to read my work. But something pushed me out of my comfort zone, and that something was having a passion that was so deep and powerful that it was more painful to sit around and do nothing than it was to go after it. (*Uncertainty be damned.*)

TAKEAWAY: Whatever you want to experience in your life—be it greater awareness, abundance, compassion, opportunity—help someone else to have more of that thing in their lives. Because whatever you do for others, you also do for yourself.

In other words, if others succeed, you succeed. And if they fail, you fail too. But the more opportunities that you offer people, the more opportunities you create for yourself. And that opens all kinds of doors to whatever you want to pursue in life.

Conclusion

The process of moving past those rejection letters and finding my own way forward has been both cathartic and life-changing. I no longer feel the uncertainty that once haunted my days, nor am I afraid to share my work with others. More importantly, I have proven to myself that I do not need anyone's permission to publish what I write. As a result, I have created a legacy of the dreams, ideas and stories that define who I am and why I do what I do.

Now, it's your turn to explore and define who you are, who you could be, and what you are capable of. So, if you take anything away from this book, let it be this:

- **You don't need permission to pursue your dreams or write your book.** You have absolute control over the life you choose, and no one can take that away from you.
- **Your story is what makes you unique, so own it.** And know that you can change your life by sharing your experiences, and the lessons that have come from them, with the right group of people.
- **The best way to overcome DØRSTOKK MILA is to immerse yourself right away in the act of creating.** Don't wait, just start.

- **Use the process outlined in this book.** Tweak it and make it your own as much as you like. What matters is that you start writing your first draft *now*, rather than putting it off for another five years.
- **Remember that no one succeeds alone, and no one fails alone.** Find those who will support you in this endeavor and distance yourself from anyone who does not—at least until you have accomplished what you set out to do.
- **Have some fun along the way!** Life is too short not to.

Another piece of advice I like to give aspiring writers is, *remember that you are not alone and that you are far better than you think*. I say this because writing is, and continues to be, challenging—no matter how long you do it. The only thing that makes it easier is reminding ourselves that even the best in the world struggle with their craft. And many of the great writers of our time have gone through the same thing themselves.

I don't know about you, but I find it reassuring that even writers who are at the top of their game—and have achieved so much success in the course of their careers—still experience the same daily pitfalls as the rest of us. And yet, each and every one of them remains committed to typing away—day after day, chapter by chapter—until they finish what they started.

You now have the ability to use storytelling as a powerful tool to open people's hearts, move others with your experiences, teach them what you have learned, and stand out from a crowded and noisy world.

Now is the time to take the first steps of your book creation journey. Get clear on what you want, then follow the process laid out in these chapters. Having used it myself many times, I can assure you that it works very well.

If you feel overwhelmed by the information presented here, remind yourself that you *will* finish your book—just take things one step at a time. But this process is only effective if you sit down and do the work. No one becomes an author by simply reading. You have to start *writing*.

That said, it is sometimes easier to work with someone who knows the ropes and can help you navigate through this process. If you become stuck at any point in your creative journey or need additional help, feel free to reach out and connect with me. I'd be happy to offer some recommendations on how to overcome any obstacle that stands between you and your path to authorship.

Whatever you do, don't waste time waiting for an opportunity to arrive at your doorstep. *Create one instead.* After all, this is *your* moment, the fulcrum of your life. Knowing what you know now, you have a choice to make: either continue to live your life as it is now, or risk leaving your comfort zone to create your legacy (and discover the writer's life along the way.)

Whatever you decide, remember that your ideas and stories deserve to be heard, and the world is eager to hear them. All you have to do is *start*.

Resources

Writing Your Book Without the Headache

DRAGON BY NUANCE
nuance.com/dragon/dragon-anywhere

This software uses machine learning to increase accuracy, allowing you to simultaneously dictate and transcribe your book, without losing your sanity. While the regular price for this software can land outside most budgets, DRAGON ANYWHERE offers a monthly subscription that falls well within an affordable range.

DESCRIPT
descript.com/transcription

This SaaS product is fast, cost-effective, accurate, powerful—taking AI-based transcription to a whole new level. It has a three-minute turnaround time for sixty minutes of audio. If you prefer human transcription, they can do that too. Simply upload your recordings, or use the real-time transcribe feature, and watch the spoken word turn into written word in a matter of minutes.

MEDIUM
medium.com

MEDIUM is a platform for writers to share their ideas with over 65 million monthly users and is excellent for overcoming any lapses in motivation. Use it to gamify your writing by breaking down specific chapters into smaller articles. You can also use these articles to build your fanbase by including a link to your book's Amazon page or to a sign-up form for your email list.

WATTPAD
wattpad.com

WATTPAD is another great platform for sharing your progress online. It allows you to build your fanbase prior to launch by leveraging its community of over 80 million avid readers. While Medium is a better fit for non-fiction writers, Wattpad is the equivalent for those who write fiction.

SCRIVENER
literatureandlatte.com/scrivener

This word-processing software was designed with aspiring authors in mind. It allows you to organize and manage all of your research, concepts, chapters and notes in one place for a streamlined workflow.

Professional Editing That Won't Break the Bank

BOOK BUTCHERS
bookbutchers.com

These editors handle everything from proofreading to line editing, while also offering content organization, sales copy revisions, plot development and pacing. Services are rendered at a very affordable price per word.

Reedsy
reedsy.com

Reedsy is a marketplace for some of the best publishing talent out there. They also offer some great resources for indie authors, including free publishing courses and book formatting software.

Bad-Ass Book Covers

Canva
canva.com

Canva is the cheapest possible Do-It-Yourself option for book covers. I have nothing against it, but many publishing experts advise investing in a professional designer instead. The rule of thumb I live by here is, do what you do best and leave the rest to a professional.

Freelance Cover Designers

There are many talented designers available for hire online. To find them, check out book covers that you like on Amazon or other book retailers. The cover designer can be found somewhere in the front or back matter, usually in the Acknowledgements section. From there, you are only a Google search away from finding the perfect cover designer for your book.

Easy-Peezy Book Formatting

REEDSY
reedsy.com

As previously mentioned, REEDSY offers free book formatting software but with limited options. Simply upload your book, choose a format and go from there.

SCRIVENER
literatureandlatte.com/scrivener

SCRIVENER also has book formatting features that you can explore.

VELLUM
vellum.pub

I am a big fan of VELLUM. It offers a variety of formatting templates and options for customization, enabling you to create a beautiful, professionally-formatted book without having to deal with the headache of hiring a designer.

Publishing (with À La Carte Options)

BOOKBABY
bookbaby.com

BOOKBABY is a self-publishing platform that offers significantly discounted ISBNs and worldwide distribution for your book. They have a pricing calculator on their site if you want to tweak and plan your publishing budget accordingly.

INGRAMSPARK

ingramspark.com

INGRAMSPARK distributes to Amazon and retailers like Barnes & Noble, independent bookstores, among others. There is a one-time setup fee of $49. It's worth noting that this platform can be tricky to navigate for new authors. If you don't know what you're doing, ask for help.

KINDLE DIRECT PUBLISHING
kdp.amazon.com

KDP is Amazon's publishing arm for distributing both e-books and print-on-demand across their USA and global marketplaces. They do not charge anything upfront, which is great if you are on a tight budget.

Book Marketing on Your Terms

AMAZON AUTHOR CENTRAL
authorcentral.amazon.com

Many new authors miss out on the easiest marketing opportunities, including forgetting to set up their AMAZON AUTHOR CENTRAL profile. This profile acts as your digital "About the Author" page and is linked to your book's retail listing on Amazon and elsewhere. It also allows you to customize your book's product page, add editorial reviews, and more.

BOOKBUB
bookbub.com

BOOKBUB is your golden ticket to reaching millions of targeted readers, if you can get it. The price to run a promotion is reasonable given the return on investment, but they are very selective about the books they choose to promote. So, be sure to read through the submission guidelines to maximize your chances of landing a spot.

BookFunnel
bookfunnel.com

Sending out ARCs (advanced reader copies) to reviewers or people on your email list seems easy enough…*at first*. However, when you consider that readers are consuming e-books on thousands of different reading devices and apps — each with its own quirks and issues — it can be exhausting to constantly troubleshoot. With BOOKFUNNEL, you can send a unique, non-shareable download link that allows reviewers to read a water-marked copy of your book, in any digital format of their choice (EPUB, MOBI, PDF, etc.)

Goodreads
goodreads.com

GOODREADS is another hidden gem for getting the word out about your book. It only takes a few minutes to set up an author profile and claim your book. From there, you can use the platform to promote and build buzz when it comes time to launch.

MailChimp
mailchimp.com

"The money is in the list." As cliché as it is, this statement is key to successful book marketing. MAILCHIMP is free for your first 2,000 email subscribers, which makes it the perfect tool for list building and marketing your book on a budget.

Substack
substack.com

For the less tech savvy, I recommend using SUBSTACK. This newsletter platform was built to save writers the hassle of having to learn the ins and outs of email marketing, so that they can focus on doing what they do best.

Done-For-You Self-Publishing

BOOKSMITH
booksmith.io

BOOKSMITH.IO brings your story to readers around the world by creating a streamlined experience that makes publishing and marketing your book both easy and profitable. Unlock your full potential with:

- Editing that reflects the finesse of a *New York Times* bestseller
- Publishing that gives your book the reach and impact it deserves
- Distribution on the shelves of major retailers and bookstores around the world
- Marketing to millions of readers to land a spot on *Amazon's Bestseller List*

Leave a Review

What Did You Think of CREATE?

Thank you for taking the time to read this book. I hope that it adds some value and quality to your creative endeavors. And if you know someone who might like it, feel free to share it with them on social media or at your next get-together.

On that note, if you enjoyed CREATE, would you mind taking a few minutes to leave a review on Amazon, Goodreads, or your favorite online bookstore?

Your honest feedback will help readers decide whether this is the right book for them. It also helps make the next edition of this book *even better*.

P.S. If you'd like a free copy of my *12-Day Book Launch*, along with more insider tips on publishing and marketing, visit: BookHip.com/MBJQHD.

About the Author

Annika is a TEDx alum, award-winning storyteller, and founder of BOOKSMITH.IO, a professional publishing company that provides indie authors with editing, design, distribution, and launch services that drive results and turn stories into bestsellers. She is best known for her motivational, high energy style of helping others create and publish content that brings their stories to life.

Over the years, Annika has worked with dozens of thought leaders and industry shakers, *New York Times* bestselling authors and Big Five Publishers. She has lived and traveled all over Europe —from Iceland to Switzerland, Norway to the UK—to learn from, and work alongside, the most innovative minds in publishing and technology.

Annika is currently based in Seattle, where she spends her time climbing, hiking, and developing technologies that make it easier and more profitable for indie authors to publish and market their books.

www.ingramcontent.com/pod-product-compliance
Lightning Source LLC
Chambersburg PA
CBHW070917080526
44589CB00013B/1334